The World of MOTORCYCLING

WORLD FAMOUS
A.J.S. PORCUPINE
500 cc
1947
NOWN SURVIVOR WITH
RIZONTAL ENGINE

The World of
MOTORCYCLING

THE MOTORCYCLE: FROM MYTH-AND-LEGEND TO NUTS-AND-BOLTS

Roland Brown

This edition published in 1997 by
Smithmark Publishers,
a division of U.S. Media Holdings, Inc.,
16 East 32nd Street,
New York,
NY 10016.

SMITHMARK books are available for bulk purchase for
sales promotion and for premium use. For details write or
call the manager of special sales, SMITHMARK
Publishers, 16 East 32nd Street, New York, NY 10016;
(212) 532-6600

Produced by Anness Publishing Limited
Hermes House
88-89 Blackfriars Road
London SE1 8HA

Printed in Singapore by Star Standard Industries Pte. Ltd.

1 3 5 7 9 10 8 6 4 2

CONTENTS

INTRODUCTION

THE WORLD OF MOTORCYCLING

Two wheels and an engine. The basic ingredients of the motorcycle are so simple; but its attraction, stronger than ever after 110 years of relentless development, is so hard to explain. Part of the reason for this is that motorcyling means so many things to so many different people. More than merely a form of transport, it incorporates everything from an ancient Scott roadster to Aprilia's modern 250cc Grand Prix racer, from a booming Velocette single to Honda's futuristic EXP-2 desert racer.

This section of the book takes a winding ride from the first ever motorcycle – Gottlieb Daimler's Einspur – to the fastest ever – Dave Campos's 322mph (518kph) Harley-Davidson – via Chelsea Bridge, Hollywood and the Nürburgring. But if it is the machines that form the outline of the motorcycling picture, then it's the people who design, build, modify, pose, commute or tour on, race, crash, repair, fight or save lives on them who add the colour.

The World of Motorcycling is their story: from Mick Doohan pulling a wheelie on his Honda NSR500 to Marlon Brando leaning on his Triumph Thunderbird; from a medical worker delivering supplies in the African Bush to a Sunday-morning superbiker cranking a Ducati 916 through a turn. Different people, on different motorcycles, and in very different situations, united by a shared appreciation of two wheels and an engine.

The Evolution of the Motorcycle

By all accounts it was a short and slow journey. With a 0.5 horsepower engine, wooden frame and no suspension, that was inevitable. But when Paul Daimler rode his engineer father Gottlieb's new contraption named Einspur — "One track"— around the countryside near Stuttgart in Germany on 10 November 1885, he was taking what is commonly accepted to be the world's first ride on a motorbike.

Bikes have come a long way from those days to the present, when even ordinary middleweights exceed 100mph (160kph) reliably and with ease. But when comparing the earliest bikes of this century to the sophisticated, powerful machines of today, in many respects it's noticeable not how much but how little motorcycles have changed. Of course, there is a huge difference between the 1901 New Werner and Honda's latest Grand Prix racer—but the two are unmistakably related. This chapter is the story of how the former evolved into the latter.

EARLY DAYS

Gottlieb Daimler wasn't much of a motorcycle man, and soon after producing Einspur in 1885 he gave up bikes to make his name in the newly-developed car industry. But Daimler had made a major breakthrough. Although steam-powered railways and ships were already well established by the 1880s, steam was ill-suited to smaller vehicles. With Einspur's 265cc internal combustion engine, Daimler, who had previously worked as an assistant to Dr Nikolaus Otto, inventor of the four-stoke engine, had shown the way forward for personal transport.

Steam-powered bikes had been tried before, notably the Michaux-Perreaux velocipede built in France in 1869, but they were gradually abandoned as petrol-burning engines gained

■ LEFT *The Werner brothers of Paris sold several hundred of their light and practical 1898 model "motocyclette" which had its engine mounted above the front wheel.*

■ BELOW *In 1901, the French firm patented the New Werner layout, with engine positioned between the wheels for improved handling, which motorcycles have used ever since.*

■ **ABOVE** *It is said that the first ever bike race took place when two motorcyclists met on the road for the first time — these two road riders certainly look to be enjoying a bit of friendly competition in 1903.*

■ **TOP** *The De Dion Bouton tricycle, powered by the same firm's reliable four-stroke single engine, was raced very successfully in the final years of the last century.*

■ **ABOVE** *Indian's single, with its engine inclined to the rear in American fashion, was very successful in 1902 – over 100 were built and there was a reported 17-year waiting list.*

■ **RIGHT** *Such was the pace of change in motorcycling's early years that Daimler's Einspur, with its huge wooden frame, was totally outclassed by bikes of 15 years later.*

popularity. Among the earliest converts were the German brothers Hildebrand, who with their partner Wolfmüller produced the world's first production motorcycle in 1894. The Hildebrand & Wolfmüller held a watercooled, 1500cc twin-cylinder four-stroke engine in a specially made steel frame. Among other high-tech features, it benefited from John Boyd Dunlop's recently invented pneumatic tyres. Its top speed of about 25mph (40kph) was quite fast enough consider-ing the rear emergency brake consisted of a simple metal bar that dragged on the ground.

The next big step in motorcycling's development came soon afterwards when two Frenchmen, Count Albert De Dion and Georges Bouton, produced a single-cylinder, four-stroke engine of about 125cc. The De Dion unit was rated at 0.5bhp but in reality produced more, revved reliably to 1800rpm, and was very compact. It was originally used to power the De Dion tricycle, which was raced successfully in the late 1890s. Frustratingly for its manufact-urers, the design was blatantly copied by

numerous other firms as motorcycle production spread across Europe.

Few of the new firms could agree on the best place to locate the engine until the Paris-based Werner brothers, whose original bike used a De Dion-style unit above the front wheel, revised their design in 1901. The New Werner's engine was placed low, between the wheels, in a steel frame, and drove the rear wheel via a leather belt. With its bicycle-style saddle, wheel-rim brakes, and improved handling due to its lower centre of gravity, the New Werner set the pattern for 20th-century motorcycle design.

■ LEFT *The Wall Autowheel, pictured here in 1910, was an engine and auxiliary wheel that clamped to a bicycle — very useful for well-laden bikes.*

■ BELOW *Lawrence of Arabia was the most famous rider of the fast and sophisticated Brough Superior V-twin of the 1920s.*

Development from that point was rapid, as enthusiasm for bike production spread across Europe and America. In that same year of 1901, Americans George Hendee and Oskar Hedstrom produced the first Indian motorbike. Three years later, as Indian was pioneering the twistgrip method of throttle control and planning its first twin-cylinder model, the firm gained a new rival named Harley-Davidson. During the next ten years, Indian, Harley and other firms including Excelsior adopted the V-twin engine layout that remains America's favourite to this day.

American firms Indian and Pierce both launched four-cylinder models as early as 1909, but by then the ultra-sophisticated four from Belgian manufacturer FN had already been on the market for four years. Benefiting from an aircooled, 363cc in-line four engine with shaft final drive, the FN was a remarkably smooth and classy device – undoubtedly an early superbike! During two decades of FN production the four's engine capacity was increased to 750cc, and further refinements including a clutch, gearbox and leading-link forks were added to the original design.

Elsewhere, too, technology was leaping ahead. By 1910 the British-built Scott featured not only a watercooled, two-stroke twin engine

■ LEFT *The world's first kick-start, situated alongside the rear wheel, was just one of the features pioneered by Yorkshire firm Scott on its two-stroke parallel twin in 1910.*

■ RIGHT *Despite some faults, Ariel's smooth Square Four of 1937 represented the pinnacle of two-wheeled sophistication before the Second World War.*

but also a kick-start, chain final drive and telescopic front forks. Early four-stroke advances included Harley's use of all-mechanically operated valves, in place of the early inlet-over-exhaust (IOE) design whereby the inlet valve was simply sucked open by the piston. In 1913, another American firm, Cyclone, produced a big V-twin roadster with overhead camshafts. Only a year later, French firm Peugeot had a vertical-twin racebike with twin cams and four-valve cylinder heads.

The American motorcycle industry suffered badly in the years after the First World War, partly due to competition from Henry Ford's ultra-cheap Model T motor car, but in Europe the bike business boomed in the 1920s. English firms such as Matchless, Triumph and Velocette, German marques BMW (whose first flat-twin, the 493cc R32, appeared in 1923) and Zündapp, and Italian manufacturers

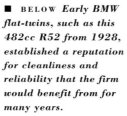

■ BELOW *Early BMW flat-twins, such as this 482cc R52 from 1928, established a reputation for cleanliness and reliability that the firm would benefit from for many years.*

Benelli and Moto Guzzi all produced a variety of increasingly sophisticated bikes.

By the late 1930s, motorcycles had evolved into reasonably fast, reliable and easily ridden machines. At the top end of the market was Ariel's Square Four, a luxurious 1000cc tourer. Triumph's 500cc Speed Twin had been launched in 1937, with a parallel twin engine layout that would serve for over 50 years. Glamorous, large-capacity V-twins were being produced by Brough and Vincent in Britain, and by Harley and Indian in America. Barely half a century after Einspur's first faltering trip, motorcycling had well and truly arrived.

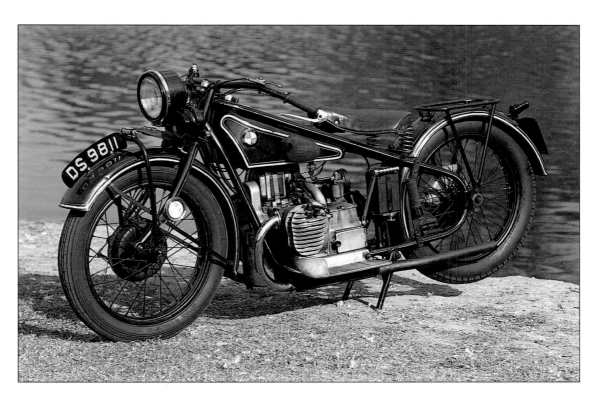

■ OPPOSITE *Several decades of progress are clear in this 1935 London Motorcycle Show publicity shot of a 500cc New Imperial with an 1897 Holden, the world's first four-cylinder bike.*

THE GOLDEN AGE

Motorcycling's rate of progress slowed considerably in the decades following the end of the Second World War. In contrast to those inventive early years, the period spanning the 1940s, 1950s and early 1960s was characterized by numerous singles and twins from the dominant British industry.

In those days, machines like the Norton Dominator, BSA Gold Star, Triumph Thunderbird and Velocette Venom ruled the road. Now these names are enough to arouse misty-eyed nostalgia for an era of blood-and-thunder biking, when traffic was light, noise regulations and speed limits were much less rigorously enforced than today's, and

motorcycling was an all-year-round pursuit whose benefits included social alienation and ingrained dirt under the fingernails.

For all the lack of revolutionary change, there was nevertheless a gradual refinement in two-wheeled design. A typical roadster of the late 1940s had no rear suspension, crude girder front forks, a bicycle-style single saddle, a manual ignition advance-retard lever, and a sluggish, low-compression engine that had been designed to run on low-octane wartime fuel. Paint finish was dull, frequently army-surplus camouflage green. Items such as a speedometer, brake light and pillion footrests were still optional extras.

■ BELOW *The Brough Superior's image and reputation for performance lived on through the 1940s and 1950s, long after production of models such as the SS100S had come to an end.*

■ RIGHT *Indian ceased production of its Chief V-twin in 1953, but the firm's subsequent attempt to produce British-style parallel twins was unsuccessful.*

Throughout the 1950s that format was modified through the adoption of brighter colours, telescopic forks, plunger and swing-arm rear suspension, speedos, dual-seats and more sophisticated electrics. Four-stroke engines adopted shorter-stroke dimensions, higher compression and aluminium barrels for added performance and reduced weight. A mid-1950s Triumph or BSA 650cc twin was good for a genuine 100mph (160kph), and handled reasonably well besides.

Britain's bike industry went from strength to strength in the 1950s, with domestic sales rising to a peak of 330,000 in 1959. The Brits

also made a big impression in America, where the home industry – suffering from poor direction and lack of small-capacity models – was in serious decline. Of the last two great American manufacturers, Indian built its final big V-twin in 1953, and Harley sold fewer than 10,000 bikes in 1955.

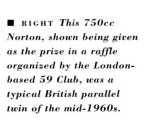

■ RIGHT *This 750cc Norton, shown being given as the prize in a raffle organized by the London-based 59 Club, was a typical British parallel twin of the mid-1960s.*

■ FAR RIGHT *Motorcycling clergyman the Reverend Bill Shergold, pictured here buying a new Triumph, founded the 59 Club and was a prominent figure during British biking's heyday in the 1960s.*

■ LEFT *These riders, far from causing trouble, are setting off from London's Trafalgar Square to deliver posters during Christian Aid week in the 1960s.*

The British firms, however, had more competition from Europe, where German firms BMW and NSU made rapid post-war recoveries. Italian manufacturers including Ducati, Gilera and MV Agusta built rapid 100 and 125cc sportsbikes that were raced in road events such as the Milano-Taranto and Giro d'Italia. Scooters also became increasingly popular, the modest performance of the Vespas and Lambrettas being offset by the advantages of weather protection and, more subjectively, style. By comparison, British small-capacity rivals, mostly powered by two-stroke Villiers engines, were considered terribly dull.

■ OPPOSITE MIDDLE *Triumph's 650cc Bonneville was the most famous British twin.*

■ OPPOSITE BELOW *Soichiro Honda, pictured (left) with co-founder Takeo Fujisawa, led Japan's assault on British dominance of the motorcycle market.*

■ RIGHT *Triumph's "bathtub" full rear enclosure, introduced on this 350cc Model 21 in 1957, was later used on bigger twins but was unpopular.*

In 1965 Honda launched the CB450 twin, which competed almost head-on with Britain's traditional parallel twins. Following hard on Honda's heels Kawasaki, Suzuki and Yamaha would soon release big motorcycles of their own – and there was nothing the British firms could do to stop the erosion of their market lead.

Italy also spearheaded the attack on British dominance on the racetrack following the introduction of the world championship series in 1949. AJS, Norton and Velocette, successful in the first few seasons, gave way to fours from Gilera and MV Agusta; in the smaller classes Moto Guzzi and Mondial battled with Germany's NSU. On the street Britain was still in the lead in the mid-1950s, but disaster was looming for firms whose complacency had led to a lack of investment and innovation.

As the 1960s arrived, it was the growing challenge from Japan that held the real danger to Britain's long-dominant industry. In 1960, Triumph boss Edward Turner made a now famous visit to several factories in Japan, returning to warn – to little avail – of what he termed as the somewhat frightening spectacle of its hugely promising and fast-growing motorcycle firms. By then Honda had already made a successful first trip to compete in the Isle of Man TT.

In the showrooms, an expanding range of well-built and sophisticated small-capacity motorcycles had been enhanced by the 50cc C100 scooter, whose famous "You meet the nicest people on a Honda" slogan would help attract annual sales of over half a million for years. Despite what many in the European industry vainly continued to believe, the Japanese would not remain content to build small bikes for long.

THE MODERN ERA

When Honda introduced the CB750 in 1969, it was not just the Japanese machine's four-cylinder, overhead-cam engine and 120mph (193kph) top speed that heralded the start of motorcycling's modern age. Equally important was the Honda's lavish specification, including an electric starter and front disc brake, and its general air of sophistication. Ironically, Triumph's three-cylinder, 750cc Trident T150, which was launched at the same time, handled at least as well and was slightly faster. But the British bike's pushrod engine, kick-start and drum brakes – plus its dubious reliability and need for frequent maintenance – marked the Triumph as a machine from an earlier era.

Japan had shown the way forward, and the 1970s would belong not just to Honda but to Kawasaki, Suzuki and Yamaha too. Kawasaki

■ LEFT *Ducati's 750 Super Sport (left) and its successor the 900SS, both singleminded race-replicas, were among the fastest and best Italian superbikes of the mid-1970s.*

■ LEFT *Honda's sophisticated CB750 four caused a sensation when it was revealed at the Tokyo Show in late 1968, and again when it was displayed at the Brighton Show shortly afterwards.*

■ BELOW *Suzuki's GS1000 of 1978 proved that the Japanese manufacturers were learning to build chassis strong enough for their mighty engines.*

■ ABOVE *Britain's crumbling hold on the bike market came under further attack in the 1970s when Triumph's Bonneville (left) was faced by Yamaha's XS650.*

■ BELOW LEFT *The Japanese firms' race to build bigger and more powerful superbikes climaxed in 1979 with the massive, six-cylinder Kawasaki Z1300.*

■ BELOW RIGHT *Moto Guzzi's 850 Le Mans Mk.1 V-twin (left) and Kawasaki's 900cc Z1 four offered contrasting brands of 1970s superbiking.*

raised the stakes again in 1973 with the launch of the 900cc Z1, whose muscular twin-cam engine gave 130mph (209kph) top speed with unburstable reliability. The bike they nicknamed the King and its descendants would dominate superbiking for much of the decade.

Not that the Japanese had it all their own way. Britain's industry might have been dying but Italy, in particular, had much to offer. Ducati and Moto Guzzi, each with a distinctive brand of V-twin engine, and Laverda, with powerful 1000cc triples headed by the legendary Jota, all produced memorable mid-1970s superbikes. The Italian bikes' biggest advantage was in handling, for the Japanese firms found chassis harder to perfect than engines. Not until the Suzuki GS1000 appeared in 1978 did Japan build a superbike

that could hold its own in the bends – and even then poor wet-weather performance remained.

Japanese manufacturers also had a "bigger is better" fixation that reached a peak in 1979 with Kawasaki's massive Z1300 six. But there were some excellent small bikes too, including Yamaha's long-running RD series of middleweight two-stroke twins. Smelly strokers fell foul of emission regulations in America, but thrived elsewhere throughout the 1980s. That decade saw Japanese aircooled fours take over the large and medium capacity market to such an extent that the term UJM – Universal Japanese Motorcycle – was coined to describe them. But there were more imaginative designs, too – notably the turbocharged models tried and then abandoned by each of what, by now, were termed as the Big Four.

■ LEFT *Ducati's 916 V-twin and Honda's 750cc V-four, the RC45, updated the two firms' traditional formats to produce stunning mid-1990s superbikes.*

■ BELOW LEFT *Kawasaki's ZZ-R1100 — the ZX-11 in America — was the world's fastest production bike for five years following its launch in 1990.*

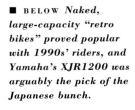

■ BELOW *Naked, large-capacity "retro bikes" proved popular with 1990s' riders, and Yamaha's XJR1200 was arguably the pick of the Japanese bunch.*

More successful 1980s' developments included the increasing fitment of fairings (and luggage systems for tourers), and the adoption of chassis features such as single-shock rear suspension and radial tyres. Aluminium became frequently used in frame construction, following the dynamic arrival of Suzuki's ultra-light GSX-R750 race-replica in 1985.

By 1990 the Japanese had almost universally adopted liquid-cooling for engines, partly to satisfy tightening emission laws. Kawasaki's awesome new ZZ-R1100 had a 16-valve engine producing over 140bhp, a twin-beam aluminium frame, a top speed of 175mph (281kph) and levels of handling, roadholding and

braking that would have been unthinkable ten years earlier. The best bikes' all-round excellence meant that developments were less dramatic than before, but outstanding machines continued to appear. Honda's CBR900RR of 1992 combined superbike power with light weight. Kawasaki's 1995-model ZX-6R challenged Honda's long-standing middleweight champion, the CBR600F, with a 160mph (257kph) top speed that few open-class bikes could better.

But not every rider simply wanted speed. From Honda's mighty Gold Wing tourer – introduced as a basic 1000cc flat-four in 1976, now a lavishly equipped 1500cc six – to scooters via sports-tourers, trail-bikes and cruisers, the Japanese built something for almost everyone. As bikes were increasingly used for leisure rather than mere transport, and the average age of riders rose to above 30 in many countries, what some bikers wanted was an unfaired retro-style machine whose appeal was based on simplicity and nostalgia.

One thing most riders seemingly did not want was technology at a premium price.

■ BELOW RIGHT *Trail bikes such as BMW's giant R1100GS have proven popular with many riders. Although most have traditionally been ridden mainly on the street, advances in technology have made trail bikes increasingly capable of handling difficult off-road terrain.*

■ BELOW *Rock star Paul Young's custom Harley-Davidson, pictured in London's King's Road, epitomizes the American machines' shift in image from outlaw hog to fashionable accessory.*

Anti-lock brakes were introduced with some success, notably by BMW. But expensive technical tours de force such as Bimota's Tesi and Yamaha's GTS1000 – each with non-telescopic front suspension – and Honda's oval-pistoned NR750 sold in small numbers.

By the mid-1990s there were increasing signs that motorcycling's balance of power was

shifting again. Japanese firms had been hard hit by the strength of the yen, which made their bikes increasingly expensive in most markets. Although the Japanese firms' engineering was stronger than ever, many models showed a lack of new ideas.

By contrast, Harley and several European manufacturers, having succeeded in matching Japanese quality, were enjoying huge success. Harley's retro-styled V-twin cruisers, BMW's sophisticated yet traditional flat-twins, reborn Triumph's classy triples and Ducati's racy V-twin sportsters offered all-important character to an increasingly image-conscious market.

INTO THE FUTURE

Futuristic concept machines appear at all the major international bike shows. With names like Morpho or Nuda, they attempt to point the way forward for motorcycle design. But while some concept-bike features do eventually make it into real life, predicting the future of the powered two-wheeler is a risky business.

In the immediate future, bikes are likely to incorporate many of the features already seen in limited numbers. Catalytic converters, fuel-injection, variable valve timing and even programmable, smart-card engine-management systems, as seen on Honda's 1994 Japanese market NSR250 race-replica, have already hit the street and seem likely to become more and more common.

Electric power has already been used for several small bikes, most promisingly by Piaggio's recent Zip & Zip scooter, which combines a petrol engine for open roads and

batteries for use in town. But current batteries are heavy, inefficient and give limited performance which would indicate that their widespread adoption in larger motorcycles is still many years away — despite the sleek,

■ ABOVE *The power characteristics of this Honda NSR250 could instantly be varied by putting a different memory card, which also acted as the ignition key, into the slot in its dashboard.*

■ LEFT *Yamaha's Morpho concept bike, pictured at the Cologne Show in 1990, had futuristic features including forkless front suspension — which was introduced on the GTS1000 two years later.*

■ LEFT *Bimota abandoned plans to compete in Grands Prix with its 500cc V-twin two-stroke, but continued to develop the engine for road-going use.*

■ BELOW LEFT *"Showdown" was Spanish student Cesar Muntada's award-winning idea of what a Harley-Davidson roadster might look like in 2020.*

Granada-Dakar Rally, Honda successfully unveiled an experimental two-stroke racer called the EXP-2, whose 402cc environment-friendly single-cylinder engine could soon be seen in a road-going form.

Bimota had earlier made headlines with the forkless Tesi, although the sales failure of this and Yamaha's GTS1000 suggests that most motorcycles' chassis will remain relatively conventional for some time. Possible chassis developments in the early 21st century include active suspension, which reacts to bumps using a computer instead of springs, a system which had already been used in the car world.

Further into the future may come hydraulic steering, tried unsuccessfully in early Tesi prototypes, two-wheel steering and two-wheel drive, which has been used with some success by off-road machines. But despite that, motorcycling's immediate future is likely to be based on more down-to-earth factors such as lightness, simplicity and individuality.

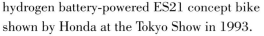

hydrogen battery-powered ES21 concept bike shown by Honda at the Tokyo Show in 1993.

More promising is the direct-injection two-stroke engine, which dramatically cuts emissions by injecting fuel directly into the combustion chamber after the exhaust port has closed, instead of allowing large amounts of unburned fuel to escape, like a conventional two-stroke. Ford has produced a prototype direct-injection car, developed in collaboration with Australian specialists Orbital, which has shown much promise.

Bimota, the small Italian firm best known for chassis engineering, produced a prototype 500cc V-twin two-stroke with direct injection in 1992, and at the time of writing finally looked set to put it into production. In the 1995

■ ABOVE *The weight and performance of batteries has so far limited their two-wheeled use, but the 1994 special "Violent Violet" was fast.*

The Rider's View

There is a lot more to motorcycling than simply riding a bike. Owning and using a motorcycle gives a different perspective on life to that of the average pedestrian or car driver. Depending on the rider, the machine and the moment, you are an individual – free, rebellious, fast-moving, glamorous, somehow above the dull troubles of the normal world. You're also mistrusted, maybe persecuted, even pitied, always vulnerable.

Those shared emotions produce a bond between motorcyclists that can sometimes bridge the huge gaps between the many different types of rider. Many's the time that the owner of a superbike has pulled up to help a novice with a broken moped. But within the overall two-wheeled scene is a vast number of diverse subgroups and cultures, reflecting the variety of experience that motorcycling has to offer.

JOIN THE CLUB

Riding a motorcycle is essentially a solitary pursuit. You sit there gripping the handlebars, peering intently ahead through visor or goggles, ears full of noise from wind and engine, mind concentrating on the road ahead. On a bike there is rarely either the time or the opportunity for conversation.

Yet motorcycling can also be a most sociable hobby. Wherever in the world there are bikes, there are riders who congregate to compare machines, modifications and cornering lines; to swap information, spare parts and tall stories. From the regulars at the Rock Store café near Los Angeles, famous weekend haunt of Harley-riding Hollywood stars including Stallone and

Schwarzenegger, and at Box Hill in Surrey, England, to Japan's Tougekozo (the "peak to peak kids"), who race their sportsbikes on mountain roads, there's a group of bikers meeting somewhere every day, and that's just the informal gatherings. There are also hundreds of official motorcycling clubs and organizations. Some are political pressure groups, notably the Brussels-based Federation of European Motorcyclists, which incorporates individual groups in over a dozen countries. Motorcycling has long been a tempting target for legislators – and riders are increasingly well organized to fight back.

Bike sport is generally run through clubs, some of which have a thriving social section. Specialist road-riding groups include Christian Bikers, Gay Bikers and Women on Wheels. Many clubs are simply locally-based organizations with a wide variety of members. One-make clubs exist for manufacturers ranging from Messerschmitt to MV Agusta. The bigger marques have national clubs in numerous countries, plus an international umbrella organization.

There are also groups for many individual models as diverse as the BSA Bantam, Honda CBX1000 and DKW rotary. Few branches of motorcycling are too obscure to have their own organization – ask the stalwarts of the Post Office Vehicle Club, or the Raleigh Safety Seven and Early Reliant Owners' Club.

■ **ABOVE LEFT** *Sportsbikes and Harleys gather every Sunday morning at the Rock Store, California's best-known bikers' meeting place.*

■ **ABOVE RIGHT** *One-make organizations such as the Norton Owners' Club offer members social events and technical assistance.*

■ **BELOW** *Members of Britain's all-party Parliamentary Motorcycle Group line up outside London's Houses of Parliament.*

Honda's Gold Wing alone supports two vast organizations in America, each with branches all over the United States, plus groups in many other countries.

The one-make club with the highest profile is the Harley Owners' Group, which has more than 250,000 members worldwide in almost 800 branches, over 500 of them in America alone. Annual gatherings at Daytona in Florida and Sturgis in South Dakota attract vast crowds, the majority on Harleys, though many of the more upwardly-mobile bikes arrive on the back of pick-up trucks these days. In many respects Harley-Davidson's claim of selling not just a motorcycle, but the lifestyle to match as well, is not an exaggeration.

MODS, ROCKERS & ANGELS

The bad boy image has been an integral part of motorcycling for years, and probably always will be. Bikes are a potent symbol of speed, rebellion and youthful aggression. And despite the ever-increasing numbers of respectable, leisure-time riders, many people still view motorcyclists as undesirable and outside the law.

In the 1960s the main cause of the bad reputation, particularly in Britain, were the Rockers. Generally dressed in studded black leather jackets, jeans and black boots, they met at cafés such as the Ace, in north London, and Johnsons, near Brands Hatch circuit in Kent, to drink tea, talk bikes and go street-racing. Favoured machinery included BSA Gold Stars,

■ LEFT *Probationary patch-club members have to earn the right to wear full colours on their backs.*

■ BELOW *The Ace Café in north London was the famous meeting-place of café racers and Rockers in the 1960s.*

Triumph Bonnevilles, Norton Dominators and the legendary Triumph/Norton hybrid the Triton, generally with tuned motors, lightened chassis and turned-down Ace handlebars.

When the Ace regulars were not racing against each other or outrunning a Daimler V-eight police car, a popular trick was to put an Elvis or Eddie Cochran single on the jukebox, then run out to the bike and attempt to complete a pre-set road circuit before the disc ended. Despite plenty of brushes with the law, the Rockers were more into bikes than violence. Even so, their bank-holiday seafront battles with their rivals the Mods – scooter riders dressed smartly in suits and anoraks – made national news regularly in the 1960s.

The Hell's Angels, whose notoriety peaked at about the same time, were a different and much more dangerous proposition. Formed in 1950 in San Bernardino, California, but later best known through the chapter based in Oakland, near San Francisco, the Angels were by far the biggest and most powerful of the many American outlaw bike groups that included Satan's

■ RIGHT *Most British café racers of the 1960s wore open-face helmets and leather jackets, and rode singles or parallel twins with low "Ace" handlebars.*

■ BELOW *A leather-jacketed Rocker is led away by a policeman after a clash with scooter-riding Mods at Margate, on England's south coast, in 1964.*

■ OPPOSITE
America's veterans of the Vietnam War have their own motorcycle club, complete with Angel-style colours and regalia.

Slaves, Gypsy Jokers and Commancheros.

Angel fever spread worldwide, and numerous chapters still exist in Europe and elsewhere. But their profile is much lower than it was in the 1960s when the Angels, famously dirty, wearing their ever-present colours – the winged-and-helmeted skull symbol – and

riding chopped Harley-Davidsons, became a feared force through clashes with police and civilians. They were immortalized in films including *Hell's Angels on Wheels* and *Hell's Angels '69*, both of which starred genuine members of the Oakland Angels, and in Hunter S Thompson's memorable book *Hell's Angels*.

■ RIGHT *The film Hell's Angels '69 starred members of the Oakland Angels, the most powerful and best-known of California's numerous groups, or "chapters".*

MOTORCYCLES IN THE MOVIES

There's no more vivid way of charting motorcycling's changing image than through its portrayal on film. Bikes have starred in the movies since the likes of *No Limit*, improbably featuring ukulele-playing George Formby at the Isle of Man TT, and *Motorcycle Squad*, about a bike cop who joins a gang of criminals, were released in the 1930s.

The most famous bike film is *The Wild One*, Stanley Kramer's 1953 classic starring Marlon Brando and Lee Marvin. Triumph-riding Brando and Harley-mounted Marvin played rival bike-gang leaders in a film loosely based on the events that occurred in 1947 at Hollister, California, where a minority of motorcyclists at a big rally caused trouble. The film was controversial enough to be banned in Britain for 15 years. It inspired teenagers, horrified their parents and formed attitudes that last to this day.

Later films featuring dubious biking characters include *The Leather Boys*, a British period piece from the 1960s, and *Girl On A*

■ LEFT *The 1930s' film* No Limit *starred George Formby as "Speed Demon" George Shuttleworth, riding his streamlined Shuttleworth Snap at the TT races.*

Motorcycle, starring Marianne Faithful. The 1960s also produced *Easy Rider*. The story featured Peter Fonda, Dennis Hopper and Jack Nicholson riding across America on a pair of chopped Harleys, complete with drugs, rednecks and music by Steppenwolf and others, and remains a classic biker film.

Another of the better efforts is the 1974 Australian production *Stone*, which features excellent street-race footage as well as outlaw gang fights. *Mad Max*, the Australian film that shot Mel Gibson to stardom in 1979, also has

■ LEFT *Jack Nicholson (left) and Peter Fonda rode a Harley across America with Dennis Hopper in* Easy Rider, *the ultimate 1960s' bike movie.*

■ ABOVE *Marianne Faithful turned plenty of heads in the 1968 film* Girl on a Motorcycle, *also released with the title* Naked Under Leather.

■ ABOVE *Marlon Brando, here with co-star Mary Murphy and his 650cc Triumph Thunderbird, caused outrage as bike-club leader Johnny in* The Wild One.

■ RIGHT *Silver Dream Racer combined a couple of songs from lead star David Essex with road-race action footage shot at Brands Hatch and Donington Park in Britain.*

its share of bike action. Other big names in films with two-wheeled interest include Mickey Rourke and Don Johnson, stars of *Harley-Davidson and the Marlboro Man*. A Harley also makes the title of the 1973 movie *Electra Glide in Blue*, which stars Richard Blake as a bike cop with an attitude problem.

Films about bike sport are headed by *On Any Sunday*, which stars Steve McQueen, already the veteran of a bike chase in *The Great Escape*, plus racers Malcolm Smith and Mert Lawwill, and conveys the thrill of dirt-track and desert racing. Robert Redford makes a fair off-road racer in *Little Fauss and Big Halsy*. Motorcycling has no road-race movies to compare with four-wheel epics such as *Grand Prix* and *Le Mans*. But both *Silver Dream Racer*, the 1979 British film starring David Essex, and *Race For Glory*, its 1989 American equivalent, include some reasonable action footage.

RIDING THE CLASSICS

Of all the two-wheeled trends of recent years, the growth of classic biking is perhaps the most dramatic. For most of the motorcycle's life, the classic concept has barely existed. To most riders, old bikes have simply been that: old bikes. Interesting and useful to a degree, but generally less desirable than the superior machines of the day.

That attitude began to change in the 1970s, as Japanese bikes took over the motorcycle market and an increasing number of enthusiasts became nostalgic for the old-fashioned, mainly British, machines of the past. The launch of *Classic Bike* magazine in 1979 reflected a growing demand, although at that time few people could have imagined the way in which interest would snowball.

These days classics are a major part of the motorcycling scene, above all in the UK. There is a wide choice of specialist magazines, each

full of advertisements from firms who sell, maintain, restore, make bits for or insure classic machinery. Complete Nortons – Manx racers and Commandos – are built from new parts. Many European dealers specialize in importing British and Japanese bikes from

■ ABOVE *Veteran machines from motorcycling's earliest years set off on the annual Pioneer Run, from London to Brighton on England's south coast.*

■ LEFT *The annual Classic Bike Show at Stafford, England has become a huge event, with club and trade stands, an autojumble, auction and concourse contest.*

■ ABOVE LEFT *Some modern-day classic riders prefer to dress in period fashion, although old-style headgear offers little protection from injury or the law.*

■ ABOVE RIGHT *Recreations of long-distance classic events such as Italy's Milano-Taranto give owners of old machines a perfect opportunity for a run.*

■ RIGHT *Demand for classics such as this Indian Chief has led to the emergence of many firms specializing in the restoration of bikes and production of spares.*

American states where the combination of consistently high sales figures and a kind climate has left clean old machines in abundance.

And there is a huge choice of events for classic bikes, too, from club runs and race meetings to shows and concourse contests. At the latter, fanatical officials dock points for a restoration that uses over-polished alloy or slightly the wrong shade of maroon on a side-panel. Bikes restored to factory standard – or, better still, with a verifiably interesting history – are highly desirable and change hands for vast sums of money.

The question of how to define a classic bike causes much heated discussion. To some hard-liners only British bikes qualify; others accept American and European machines too. One of the fastest-growing organizations of all is the Vintage Japanese Motorcycle Club, which caters for owners of Japanese bikes over 15 years old and has more than 4,000 members.

Things are more precisely defined for really old bikes, for which long-running organizations such as the Vintage Motor Cycle Club have established rules. Veteran bikes are defined by the VMCC as those built before 1915; vintage as made between 1915 and 1930; and post-vintage as between 1931 and 1945.

At the other end of the scale are those riders who prefer their classics straight out of a crate. Most current Harley-Davidson models, the glut of Japanese retro-bikes and Triumph's 1995-model Thunderbird – complete with traditional mouth-organ tank badge and peashooter silencers – combine the advantages of modern engineering with the look and at least some of the nostalgic appeal of the originals.

LEARNING TO RIDE

For many motorcyclists, learning to ride a bike involved wobbling off on a two-wheeler for the first time, possibly on a private training-ground with a road-safety instructor on hand to impart the basics of throttle and brake control. But these days, with bikes ever-faster and roads increasingly crowded, more advanced forms of two-wheeled tuition have become popular.

■ BELOW *Many sports-bike riders take advantage of the advanced courses that help reveal the secrets of Germany's uniquely demanding Nürburgring circuit.*

Some of these take place on the road, in the form of expert-level instruction along the lines of that given to police motorcyclists. The course run by the London-based Metropolitan Police combines vital safety tuition with spirited road riding and is considerably more exciting – and probably more beneficial – than the more conventional advanced driving courses.

But it is the racetrack where the majority of motorcyclists go to learn how to ride fast and safely – or simply for an excuse to blast round at high speed with no fear of police radar traps, or of traffic coming in the opposite direction. Road-racing schools take place at circuits as far apart at Laguna Seca in California, Donington Park in England and Germany's Nürburgring, often with a fleet of identical, race-prepared bikes available for use by the students.

Best-known of the American set-ups is the California Superbike School run by Keith Code, a former national-level racer who counts among his former students Grand Prix stars Eddie Lawson, Wayne Rainey and Doug Chandler. Keith Code's analytical approach to controlling a motorcycle at speed, outlined in videos and books including *A Twist of the Wrist,*

■ OPPOSITE *In many countries professional training is now compulsory before a novice motorcyclist takes to the road for the first time.*

has helped many motorcyclists to ride at high speeds more safely.

Germany's famous old Nürburgring course, with its 72 bends in 13 miles (20 kilometres) of snaking, armco-lined tarmac, presents a very different challenge. For much of the year the Ring is a public road, which any vehicle can use on payment of a few Deutschmarks. But the circuit also hosts intensive riding courses, some lasting for several days, at which track experts pass on their hard-won knowledge.

The final part of a typical three-day course is a single assessment lap for each pupil, marked by a team of instructors who hide in the bushes at key points around the track. Pass that exam with a perfect score, and on Ring open days you might stand a chance of keeping up with the Porsche factory testers or even the locals who also make frequent use of the circuit.

■ ABOVE *Few pupils have the time or energy to admire the scenery during off-road riding schools such as the one held in Wales by enduro star Geraint Jones.*

■ LEFT *Many road-race schools, including the Yamaha-sponsored one at Donington Park, provide bikes and clothing as well as expert tuition from leading riders.*

THE GEAR

Modern motorcycle clothing is almost as sophisticated as the bikes themselves. These days a serious rider wears a full-face helmet made from lightweight composite materials, and brightly-coloured, one-piece protective leathers. The well-dressed motorcyclist is likely to draw some suspicious looks if found wandering around on foot.

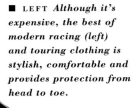

■ LEFT *Although it's expensive, the best of modern racing (left) and touring clothing is stylish, comfortable and provides protection from head to toe.*

■ ABOVE *Marlon Brando's role in the controversial movie* **The Wild One** *stamped the image of a tough biker in jeans and black leather jacket on the public consciousness.*

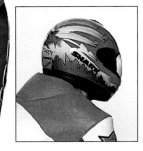

■ ABOVE *This leather suit's neck hump, designed to smooth the air-flow, gives a tiny speed increase to a 125cc racer but is of dubious benefit for road use.*

■ ABOVE *A two-piece touring suit usually has a zip to hold jacket and trousers together, reducing draughts and increasing protection.*

Riding gear was very different in biking's early years, when motorcyclists wore cloth caps and tweed jackets, just as they had for riding the bicycles from which many early machines were developed. Before the Second World War many riders' kit comprised nothing more specialized than a back-to-front cap and pair of goggles. Others would wear a leather flying helmet, and maybe a leather trenchcoat, heavy leather gauntlets and thick boots.

After the War, motorcyclists began to adopt a uniform of ex-airforce flying jackets and boots, with various items of army-surplus clothing being used for bad-weather gear. Crash

■ RIGHT *Modern off-road and bad-weather riding gear makes use of man-made fabrics such as Goretex and Kevlar to provide strength and weather protection.*

■ BOTTOM *The black leather jacket is the classic biker uniform — often customized with badges, patches, lettering and studs.*

■ ABOVE *Geoff Duke was among the first of the racers to wear wind-cheating one-piece leathers in the 1950s.*

Leather suits became increasingly popular in the 1970s. Full-face helmets were common by then but their easily-scratched visors made night riding difficult, and waterproofs that lived up to their name were rare.

By the 1990s full leathers were commonplace among serious riders, with many firms offering wide ranges of colourful one- and two-piece designs. Many modern suits incorporate sophisticated body armour; racers and some road riders wear spine-protectors too. Helmets feature sophisticated air vents and long-lasting anti-scratch visors.

Bad-weather clothing ranges from simple unlined waterproofs to elaborate suits, made from breathable, man-made fibres, featuring high-visibility reflective patches, detachable linings and padding of their own. In cold weather riders can switch on electrically heated gloves, vests or full suits. Modern motorcycling gear isn't cheap, but the best of it is extremely effective.

■ ABOVE *Before the Second World War bike riders usually wore goggles, a cap, a coat, leather gauntlets and a pair of stout shoes.*

helmets, which had been used for racing since the 1930s, became more common among road riders, and the early leather-sided pudding-basin design was gradually superseded by a more protective open-face style.

Black leather jackets were popular with American motorcyclists by the early 1950s, and hit the big time with the release of *The Wild One* in 1953. Marlon Brando's character Johnny, in his turned-up jeans and double-breasted Schott jacket, epitomised this classic style along with James Dean, Elvis and others. Over the years the basic item has been added to and modified with various tassels, patches, badges and metal studs, but its essential appeal – and attitude – remains.

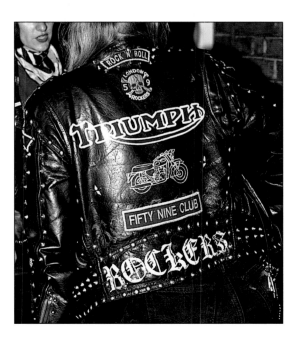

TOURING

Motorcycle touring means different things to different people. From a gentle weekend trip to an epic journey around the world; from a professionally planned expedition involving dozens of riders, to the result of one person's sudden urge simply to get on a motorbike and ride. The beauty of touring by motorbike is that the journey itself is as much a part of the experience as the stops.

■ BELOW *Big cruisers are not the most comfortable or practical way to travel, but they can cover long distances enjoyably if you don't mind taking your time.*

With its unique ability to cover reasonably large distances while immersing its rider in his or her surroundings, the motorcycle is perfect for explorers. Ted Simon, author of *Jupiter's Travels*, the best-selling story of a four-year trans-world ride on a 500cc Triumph twin in the 1970s, wrote of his gut feelings about how he wanted to travel. He instinctively knew his transport had to be a motorcycle, even though he had neither bike nor licence before planning his trip.

Simon chose the Triumph Tiger partly out of patriotism and partly because it was fairly light while relatively simple and solid – a positive boon when it came to repairs. Similar thinking has led many more recent two-wheeled explorers to use single-cylinder trail bikes such as Honda's XL600 and Yamaha's XT600 Ténéré. Others accept the extra weight of BMW's long-running boxer twins, notably the dual-purpose R80 and R100GS models, to gain the benefits of increased comfort and shaft final drive. Husband and wife team Richard and Mopsa English also opted for an old

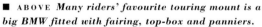

■ ABOVE *Many riders' favourite touring mount is a big BMW fitted with fairing, top-box and panniers.*

■ RIGHT *Norway provides tourers with some excellent roads, and breathtaking views.*

■ BELOW *Ireland's charm makes it a great country for touring, and a big slow-revving Moto Guzzi California is an ideal bike on which to travel.*

Triumph twin for the round-the-world trip described in their book *Full Circle*, but they added a large sidecar too.

Choosing the basic motorcycle is merely the first step in preparing for a very long tour, particularly one through difficult terrain. Any bike will require modification, notably to enable it to carry the large amount of luggage necessary. Solid fibreglass or preferably aluminium panniers may be fitted, in conjunction with soft luggage of leather, plastic or canvas. Many riders fit home-made metal racks that hold cans for spare fuel and water. Other common modifications include large-capacity fuel tanks, oil-coolers and protective engine bash-plates, extra fuel filters and heavy duty wheel-rims and spokes.

Purpose-built tourers such as Honda's Gold Wing, Yamaha's Venture or Harley's Electra Glide make life easier with fairings, big seats and easily detachable luggage facilities, and often provide accessories such as stereos, electrical sockets, cruise control and foot-boards. But small and apparently unsuitable bikes can be used successfully – provided factors such as route, daily distances and luggage are chosen accordingly.

Riders wishing to venture further afield without the time and expense of buying, preparing and possibly transporting a bike can turn to a growing number of specialist firms. Some offer just bike hire, but many provide complete motorcycling package tours for which the cost usually includes a local guide, food and accommodation, plus a following vehicle to carry excess luggage and deal with problems. Whether you want to ride a BMW in the Alps, a Harley-Davidson across America or an Enfield Bullet through India, there is a firm that can arrange it.

Several manufacturers have seen the potential for organized excursions, too. Honda's Transalp Rallies provided a good excuse for European owners to test their XL600Vs' dual-purpose ability, and Honda has also arranged longer, more road-oriented trips for the ST1100 sports-tourer. Harley-Davidson tours have included an 80-strong excursion to Norway's Nordkapp, deep inside the Arctic Circle. Best of all were the series of Spirit of Adventure trips organized by Yamaha for owners of Ténéré and Super Ténéré trail-bikes. These were demanding treks, in Egypt, Mexico, America and Australia, which gave owners the opportunity to ride through harsh and often beautiful terrain, with organization, riding gear, machinery and back-up – including a medical helicopter – taken care of.

None of those things is necessary for an average bike tourer, whose trip maybe lasts for two weeks in Europe or America and is all on tarmac roads. Most medium or large-capacity bikes can be pressed into service for an annual touring holiday, merely with the addition of a tank-bag, a set of throw-over panniers and perhaps a rucksack either worn by the pillion passenger or strapped to the empty seat.

■ RIGHT *A tank-bag and pair of throw-over panniers can transform even a simple unfaired roadster such as Triumph's Trident 900 into a capable tourer.*

■ BELOW *Yamaha's series of Spirit of Adventure trips gave owners of the firm's trail bikes the opportunity to ride them in remote places such as central Australia.*

Motorcycles and their Anatomy

Few motorcyclists are prepared simply to ride their bikes and leave them alone the rest of the time. Most riders are enthusiasts, far more knowledgeable about their machines than the average car driver. The majority positively enjoy maintaining, tuning, customizing or adapting their bikes in some way, whether to improve performance, enhance looks or to make theirs different from everyone else's.

In the early years regular work was absolutely unavoidable, as bikes were mostly used as a cheap form of transport, and needed frequent maintenance that in most cases only the rider was able to provide. As bikes improved, and basic servicing was increasingly carried out by professionals, keen owners could always think of ways to improve their machines. Even now, with standard bikes better and more reliable than ever before, the opportunity to spend large amounts of time and money on them is undiminished.

CAFÉ RACERS AND SPECIALS

Specials are arguably the most exciting and glamorous bikes of all. The term essentially means something hand-built, either a one-off or a small series of similar machines. Some are notable mainly for their unusual design – bikes with two engines or radical suspension, some created as much for the engineering challenge as for pure performance. But most specials are built for speed, and that certainly goes for café racers. The tuned-up sportsbike with low handlebars and a single seat remains one of motorcycling's most vivid images.

BSA's Gold Star Clubman of the late 1950s and early 60s was arguably the first café racer, although the legendary 500cc single was not

■ ABOVE *In 1974, when superbike riders wore open-faced helmets and flared jeans, Dunstall's Honda and Kawasaki fours were among the ultimate café racers.*

■ LEFT *The most successful 1960s special was the Triton, a fast and fine-handling blend of Triumph parallel twin engine and Norton Featherbed frame.*

■ BELOW *Some specials,
such as this four-cylinder
Triumph powered by a
side-by-side pair of
750cc Bonneville
engines, are built more
for show than for go.*

■ RIGHT *BSA's 500cc
Gold Star, complete
with "Ace" handlebars
and filterless Amal
carburettor, had few
rivals as a café racer
during the early 1960s.*

■ BELOW *The
handsome red special
built by German firm
AMC was among the
best of many recent
sportsbikes powered by
Harley-Davidson's
V-twin engine.*

actually a special but a standard factory-built model. Twins from BSA, Norton and Triumph took over in the 1960s, and were frequently modified with clip-on handlebars, rear-set footrests, alloy fuel tanks and free-breathing exhaust systems. Many parts were provided by engineers such as Paul Dunstall, whose Norton-powered Dunstall Dominator was a 1960s classic.

The archetypal café racer was the Triton, the blend of Triumph engine and Norton Featherbed frame that gave the best of British power and handling. Some riders combined Triumph motor and BSA chassis to form a Tribsa, or housed a Vincent V-twin engine in a Featherbed frame to produce the exotic Norvin.

The era of the café-race special continued when Japanese bikes took over in the 1970s. Honda's CB750 and then Kawasaki's Z900 and Z1000 provided seemingly endless four-cylinder horsepower, but early models were let down by their handling. Established British chassis specialists such as Dresda and Dunstall, plus others including Rickman, Harris, Fritz Egli from Switzerland, Bimota of Italy and Georges Martin from France, developed racy chassis kits for the big fours.

Engine tuning also featured highly in the café-racer cult over the years. State-of-the-art motors progressed from Bonneville lumps with ported heads and open-mouthed Amal carbs, via Yoshimura-tuned GS1000 Suzukis to modern turbocharged Kawasaki ZZ-R1100s. Harley-Davidson's long-standing lack of a sportsbike led to dozens of firms building V-twin sportsters of their own in a variety of styles.

■ BELOW *By far the most popular custom bike powerplant is Harley-Davidson's V-twin, here used to good effect by Dutch chassis specialist Nico Bakker.*

CUSTOM CYCLES

To some riders, the way a bike looks is far more important than the way it rides. A motorcycle can be an art form – a sculpture on two wheels – a chrome-plated, custom-painted, elaborately engraved celebration of style and individuality that may be difficult to control due to over-long forks, a hard-tail rear end, a massively wide rear tyre or a combination of all three.

The best custom bikes, built by visionaries such as California-based legend Arlen Ness, challenge existing concepts with intricate engineering and new images. Their influence can be seen in the thousands of less radical customized bikes at Daytona Beach or Sturgis, each sporting aftermarket parts chosen to make a machine stand out from the crowd.

Ironically, the custom movement began in America in the 1940s and 1950s when Harley riders began to strip their bikes of unnecessary accessories, mainly in search of improved performance, to produce machines known as bobbers. Modifying the chassis by kicking out the front forks for extra stability became popular, and in the 1960s this was increasingly taken to extremes with longer and longer forks,

■ RIGHT *Much of a custom bike's appeal is in the quality of its finish, and paintwork is often done by experts such as Californian Jeff McCann.*

■ BELOW *The Harley ridden by Peter Fonda in* Easy Rider, *with its ape-hanger bars, long forks and lack of front brake, summed-up the late 1960s custom style.*

often holding a bicycle-thin front wheel with no brake. The classic late 1960s custom was the chopped Harley with high, pull-back handlebars, massively extended forks and hard-tail (ie, unsprung) rear end, as ridden by Peter Fonda's character, Captain America, in the film *Easy Rider*.

In the mid-1970s Ness, who had progressed from painting bikes to building complete machines, was central in popularizing a new custom look, with lower handlebars, short forks and a long, low-slung chassis reminiscent of a drag-racer's. Ness's Bay Area style (his shop was in San Leandro, near San Francisco)

■ BELOW *Sometimes custom bikes are treated as art, as when British customizer Uncle Bunt's Yamaha formed part of a Birmingham exhibition in 1994.*

■ ABOVE *Harley-Davidsons are frequently referred to as hogs, but this customized V-twin looks as though it would be more at home in a cattle market.*

■ BELOW *For those who don't like fancy paint and shiny chrome, building a ratbike provides the perfect opportunity to let the imagination run wild.*

normally centred on a tuned Harley V-twin engine with open-mouthed carburettors, intricate exhaust pipes and names like Kwik Silver, Accel Bike and Strictly Business. Harleys have always been the most popular bikes for customizing, with Honda's CB750 making an impression in the 1970s and Triumph twins retaining a loyal following.

That remains true today, as Harley-Davidson itself has recognized in recent years with a wide variety of niche models and an array of factory accessories. Specialist customizing shops have thrived, too, offering everything from chrome-plated footpegs to hard-tail frames and complete machines. And although most modern custom bikes are merely Harleys with a few bolt-on parts, there will always be individuals dedicated to building motorcycles with a radical and eye-catching look.

SIDECARS AND TRIKES

Many modern motorcyclists regard sidecars as strange contraptions that lack both the motorbike's advantages of mobility and performance, and the car's benefits of comfort and convenience. In these days of relatively cheap cars, it certainly is difficult to make a logical argument for three-wheeled travel. But both sidecars and three-wheelers are still popular – albeit with a minority – not for practical reasons but simply because they are different and fun.

The three-wheeler's attraction has traditionally been more down-to-earth. Very early examples included Edward Butler's pioneering Petrol-Cycle of 1888. In the 1920s, three-

■ LEFT *This BSA's large sidecar provided generous, fairly weather-proof and relatively cheap transportation in 1924, when the outfit was employed as a taxi.*

■ FAR LEFT *Many solo riders consider sidecars rather dull, but they can provide plenty of entertainment, even when bolted to a humble 500cc BSA trials bike.*

■ BELOW *A Princess sidecar was a popular addition to Indian's Chief V-twin in 1936, and treated its passenger to a leather seat and a very comfortable ride.*

transport was a big single-cylinder Panther bike weighed down by an enormous double-adult unit alongside, loaded with children. The same decade saw the bubble cars, tiny enclosed three-wheelers made by firms including German aircraft manufacturers

wheelers such as the Morgan and Coventry Victor, generally with two wheels up front and one behind, offered good performance at a low price and even led some observers to predict that they would take over from bikes altogether. In the 1930s the opposite layout became more popular in America, where Indian's Despatch Tow and Harley's Servicar – basically a 45ci model with a large box between two rear wheels – served as small-scale pick-up trucks.

In Britain the sidecar's popularity peaked in the 1950s, when the typical mode of family

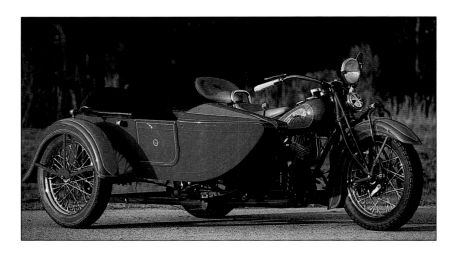

■ BELOW *Custom trikes powered by big V-eight car engines are a frequent sight at gatherings such as Daytona — for some owners, the bigger the better.*

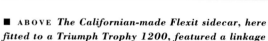

■ ABOVE *The Californian-made Flexit sidecar, here fitted to a Triumph Trophy 1200, featured a linkage system that allowed it to lean with the bike in bends.*

Heinkel and Messerschmitt. Cheap cars spelt the beginning of the end for three-wheeled travel by the 1960s. But machines such as the Bond Bug and Reliant Robin, increasingly car-like in looks if not stability, were produced for some years afterwards.

These days the only three-wheelers still in production are enthusiasts' machines, such as the Triking, whose transverse V-twin Moto Guzzi engine, exposed between two front wheels, gives the look of an early Morgan. Other idiosyncratic offerings along similar lines are the JZR, powered by Honda's CX500 V-twin, and the Lomax, which uses the engine, chassis and suspension from Citroen's 2CV car. More upmarket is the sporty Grinnall Scorpion, whose four-cylinder BMW K1100 engine gives a top speed of 130mph (208kph).

True sidecars remain popular in Continental Europe, especially Germany, where fully-enclosed and often lavishly equipped modern devices can be seen alongside colour-matched superbikes such as Honda's CBR1000 or Yamaha's FJ1200. Among the most exotic is the Krauser Domani, a futuristic and expensive BMW-powered device that resembles a Grand

Prix kneeling sidecar. Perhaps the most unlikely – and exciting – is the Flexit, a Californian creation whose linkage system allows bike and sidecar to lean in parallel through corners, in similar fashion to the Flxicar racers of the 1920s.

BELOW *In the 1920s, when it was not done for a young lady to ride pillion, a chap's best hope was to fit his Triumph with a Gloria sidecar.*

ARMY BIKES

The motorcycle's speed and manoeuvrability has made it an important tool in wartime, and the "iron horse" has been used to good effect from the First World War to recent times. Bikes of many types and nationalities have been converted for fighting use with camouflage paint schemes, modifications for extra strength and reliability, and even fitment of machine-guns – sometimes in a sidecar alongside, some-times on a solo for use by the rider alone.

British forces in the First World War used a variety of bikes, mainly for reconnaissance and communications work. Triumph supplied the Army with 30,000 units of its three-speed Model H; Douglas built almost as many of its sturdy horizontal twin; and P&M supplied the Royal Flying Corps with its 3.5bhp, two-speed single. German forces also used bikes, notably after production of the four-cylinder Belgian

FN had been taken over by the occupying German Army.

Germany's best-known bike in the Second World War was the BMW R75, which normally came fitted with a sidecar and later starred in many war films. Moto Guzzi also produced several military models such as the Alce and

■ ABOVE *A Canadian rider and his Harley WLC are the centre of youthful interest in 1941, in the grounds of an English country house used as a Brigade headquarters.*

■ LEFT *These British Army riders, splashing their single-cylinder machines through a ford, are taking part in a training exercise in Essex in 1941.*

■ LEFT *This captured Second World War BMW flat-twin and sidecar gave three British RAF mechanics the chance of a ride at Sidi Rezegh, Libya in 1942.*

■ RIGHT *BSA's M20 was useful for delivering copies of an Army newspaper to South African troops based in a remote part of the Western Desert in 1942.*

■ LEFT *A military bike enthusiast poses in suitable attire with his neatly restored Triumph Model C, built in 1914 and a veteran of the First World War.*

humble motorbike. Harley-Davidson's 350cc military machine, powered by a single-cylinder Rotax two-stroke engine, is exported to forces including the British Army. Basically a sturdy trail bike with panniers around its front wheel and a rifle rack on the back, the Harley is mainly used for reconnaissance work and convoy duties. Its predecessor, the 500cc Armstrong, played a role in the Gulf War, as did Italian-made Cagivas and Husqvarnas.

Airone, which were flat-singles of 500 and 250cc. The bigger bike often dragged a sidecar, and was also made as a three-wheeler called the Trialce. An early predecessor of Guzzi's current transverse V-twin engine was used to power a small armoured car.

Most of the bikes produced for the Second World War were simple 350cc singles from Matchless, Norton and Triumph, but the best-known Allied bikes were the American-made V-twins: Indian's 500cc Model 741 Military Scout and Harley's 750cc WLA 45. The Harley, in particular, was churned out in huge numbers – at one point in 1942 the Milwaukee factory was building 750 a week, for use by Russian and Chinese armies as well as by the Americans, Canadians and British. After the war many ex-army 45s were converted to civilian use, and did much to increase Harley's worldwide popularity.

Even in these days of ultra-sophisticated weaponry, many forces still have a role for the

■ BELOW *French Army troops, waiting for embarkation orders at a British port in June 1944, on Harleys with rifles mounted alongside the front wheel.*

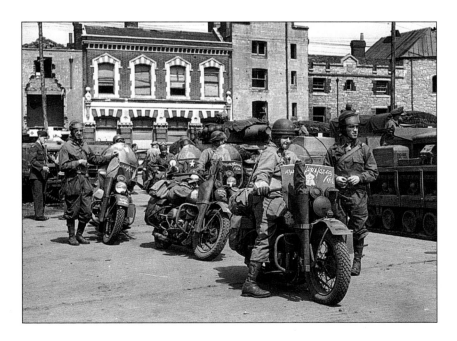

THE MOTORCYCLE AT WORK

For many riders motorcycling is not just a hobby but a job. Bikes are used for a variety of work – in most cases because their combination of open-road speed and ability to cut through traffic is unmatched by any other form of transport. The attraction of being paid to ride a bike draws many enthusiastic motorcyclists to try despatch riding, although for many the reality of riding all day in all weathers fails to match the dream. Some riders in cities around the world have found alternative employment as a two-wheeled taxi service whose journey times beat those of any conventional cab.

Police motorcyclists are some of the most visible two-wheeled workers, and use a huge variety of specially adapted bikes. Best known is the Harley-Davidson V-twin, as used by American forces for many years, including in a lead role in the film *Electra Glide in Blue*.

■ LEFT *The comfort, performance and reliability of BMW's boxer twins helped make them popular with police forces in many countries for years.*

■ LEFT *American forces, such as the California Highway Patrol, have traditionally used Harleys, although Kawasaki fours were popular in the 1980s.*

■ ABOVE LEFT *Grand Prix stars and Riders for Health charity workers Randy Mamola (hidden, left) and Kevin Schwantz (right) visit Lesotho in 1992.*

■ ABOVE RIGHT *Many national organizations such as Britain's Post Office run fleets of small-capacity bikes, like Honda's single-cylinder RS250, for city-centre use.*

■ FAR RIGHT *Despatch riders are a familiar sight on many city streets, normally loaded with luggage and carving through the traffic with practised ease and confidence.*

Traditionally a large-capacity road model converted with a single seat, radio equipment, extra identification lights, first-aid kit, fire extinguisher and weather protection, the police bike often ends up being rather heavy – although small bikes are commonly used for urban duties.

Almost every major manufacturer produces at least one model aimed at the lucrative police force market. Among the most common have been the Triumph Saint 650cc parallel twin of the 1960s; the Kawasaki Z1000 four that was popular in America in the 1980s and featured in the popular *CHiPs* television series about the California Highway Patrol; and the BMW flat-twin, which in various guises has been in police use, in Germany and other countries, for many decades.

Other two-wheeled workers include those from the motoring rescue services, whose first response to a breakdown call is often by bike, and the organizations that transport blood and other urgently needed medical supplies to hospitals. Motorcycling paramedics, carrying a wide range of life-saving equipment, can often reach road-crash or heart-attack victims before an ambulance – sometimes with life-saving results. It has been known for local midwives to find mopeds or motorcyles to be the quickest and most efficient way to travel.

Motorcycles also perform a vital service in less developed countries, where they provide otherwise impossible mobility to health workers and teachers. Riders For Health, the motorcycling charity backed by leading Grand Prix racers including Randy Mamola, works in African countries teaching local riders how to use and maintain their machines so that they can reach remote areas whenever needed.

■ RIGHT *Motorcycling paramedics can reach emergencies quickly on machines such as this Norton rotary, fitted with a variety of life-saving equipment.*

ANATOMY OF A MOTORCYCLE

A motorcycle's essential ingredients may simply be two wheels and an engine, but its design can go in any direction from there. Bikes vary from the latest Grand Prix missile to the earliest roadster; from a high-tech sports-tourer to a humble commuter machine. Over the years motorcycles have been powered by batteries, by rockets, even by the sun. They have used vastly different frames, bodywork, suspension, seating and engine positions.

But that's only a tiny minority, and most motorbikes are essentially very similar. Since the New Werner in 1901, the predominant layout of motor and riding position has been unchanged. Piston engines, in both two-stroke and four-stroke form, have powered the vast majority of bikes since even before then. A handful of basic systems has been adapted and updated over the years to provide suspension, braking, roadholding, and sometimes weather-protection or luggage-carrying ability.

The days when all motorcyclists needed to be knowledgeable about the workings of their temperamental machines are gone. Modern techno-logy and production efficiency ensures that most modern bikes are reliable, oil-tight and require minimal maintenance. They increasingly feature sophisticated electronics, engine-management systems and parts requiring specialist tools – so it's not surprising that many modern riders rely on a professional for all but the most simple mechanical work. But beneath the neon-coloured plastic and the manufacturers' publicity claims, most bikes work in much the same way they have for years.

Ducati's World Superbike racing championships have played a big part in the firm's recent sales success

Removing the cover reveals a pillion seat — and unusually for a sports-bike, the 900SS has a passenger grab-rail too

Ducati's tubular steel ladder frame uses the engine to add rigidity

Like the front forks, the single shock absorber is made by Japanese specialist Showa, and is adjustable for spring preload plus both compression and rebound damping

The cantilever style aluminium swing-arm operates the shock unit directly, rather than via a rising-rate linkage as used by many modern bikes

A small single brake disc is adequate at the rear, as forward weight transfer under hard braking makes the back wheel lock up very easily

Tyres are both low-profile radials, the rear being much wider than the front to cope with the forces of acceleration

Twin silencers are large to meet strict noise limits — although the 900SS retains Ducati's traditional V-twin exhaust note

■ BELOW *Ducati's 900SS, here with the lower part of its fairing removed, combines the Italian marque's traditional V-twin engine and tubular steel frame with many features typical of a modern sportsbike.*

Handlebars are set low to give a wind-cheating riding position

Fairing and screen protect the rider from the elements, and help give a top speed of over 135mph (216kph) despite the engine's fairly modest 80bhp output

A large airbox is crucial to engine performance, with the result that much of what looks like a large fuel tank contains only air

Twin Mikuni carburettors are situated in the crook of the engine's Vee

The Ducati's fork angle, or rake, is 25 degrees — fairly steep, to give quick and light steering, but not dramatically so by modern sportsbike standards

Front forks are the "upside-down" type currently fitted to most sports machines, with the thicker and more rigid outer section at the top

Twin discs are large at 320mm in diameter, can "float" on their mountings to allow for expansion when hot, and are gripped by four-piston calipers whose large pad area provides maximum braking power

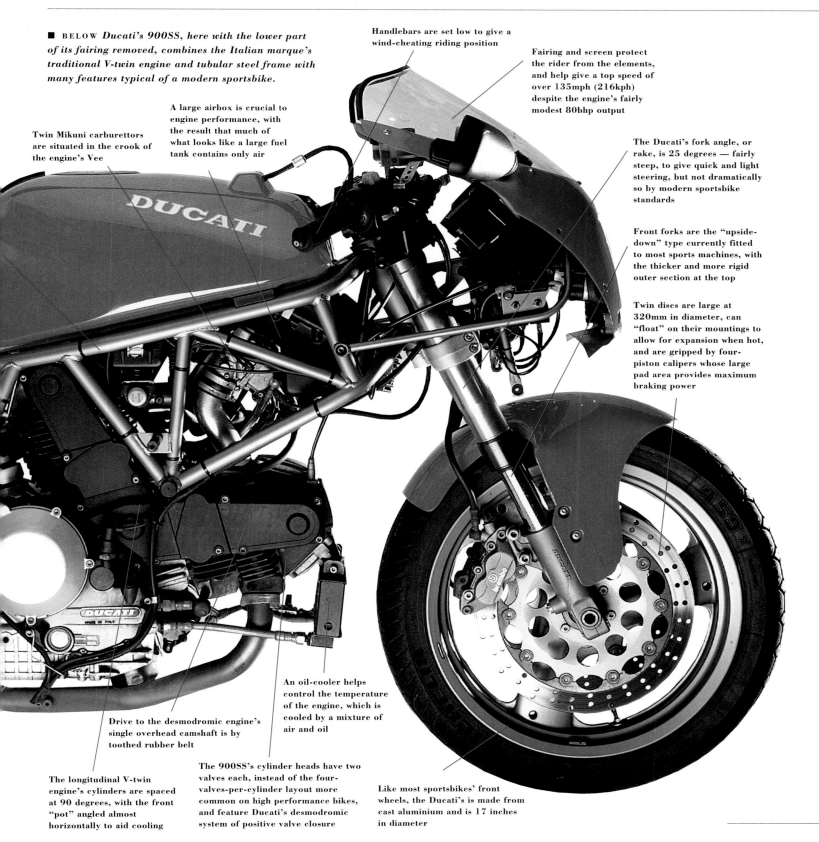

An oil-cooler helps control the temperature of the engine, which is cooled by a mixture of air and oil

Drive to the desmodromic engine's single overhead camshaft is by toothed rubber belt

The longitudinal V-twin engine's cylinders are spaced at 90 degrees, with the front "pot" angled almost horizontally to aid cooling

The 900SS's cylinder heads have two valves each, instead of the four-valves-per-cylinder layout more common on high performance bikes, and feature Ducati's desmodromic system of positive valve closure

Like most sportsbikes' front wheels, the Ducati's is made from cast aluminium and is 17 inches in diameter

Anatomy of a Motorcycle

SUCK-SQUEEZE-BANG-BLOW

The four-stroke engine is named after its four basic operations: induction, compression, combustion and exhaust. Invented by Dr Nikolaus Otto and also known as the Otto Cycle, the four-stroke principle has been motorcycling's mainstay throughout this century. While such elements as valve train

■ RIGHT *This four-cylinder, 16-valve cylinder head from BMW's K1 is disassembled to show its twin camshafts and valves, their springs and the "buckets" operated by the camshaft lobes.*

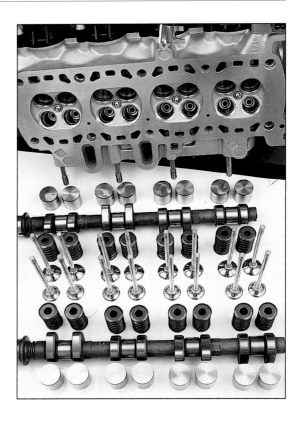

THE FOUR-STROKE CYCLE

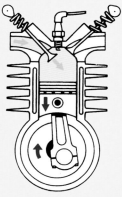

1 INDUCTION (SUCK)
As the piston descends, the inlet valve opens, allowing fuel/air mixture to be drawn into the cylinder

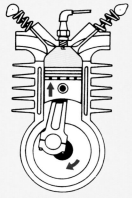

2 COMPRESSION (SQUEEZE)
The inlet valve then closes and the piston travels upwards, compressing the mixture

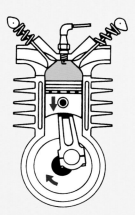

3 COMBUSTION (BANG)
Just before the piston reaches the top of its stroke (known as Top Dead Centre), the spark plug ignites the compressed fuel/air mixture, forcing the piston down on its power stroke

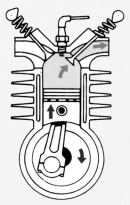

4 EXHAUST (BLOW)
As the piston rises again the exhaust valve opens, allowing the burnt gases to be released through the exhaust port

design and materials used have changed greatly since early motors that produced just a few horsepower, the basic suck-squeeze-bang-blow sequence remains the same.

Road-going four-stroke multis now run reliably to as high as 15,000rpm, and provide phenomenal performance. The best Japanese four-cylinder 600cc engines deliver 100bhp, more than most car units, while the biggest bikes are so powerful that in many countries their 140bhp-plus motors have to be restricted for legal purposes.

■ **TYPES OF FOUR-STROKE ENGINE**

The earliest and simplest four-stroke layout, the single, dominated in the 1950s and is still used for various motorcycles ranging from mopeds to racebikes. In spite of increasingly

■ RIGHT *On this cut-away of Honda's CBR600F it is possible to follow how air travels from the duct above the front wheel to the airbox, through the air-filter and carburettors to the engine, and then out via the exhaust system. Note also the cross-section of the steel frame beams visible at the steering head.*

sophisticated balancing arrangements, its practical limit remains about 650cc. Parallel twins took over in the 1960s, and can be used in either 360-degree — both pistons rising together — or 180-degree layouts. BMW's classic flat-twin, or boxer, layout is generally smoother and ideal for cooling, if not for ground-clearance. V-twins vary in the angle of their cylinders, and can be longitudinal, like the 45-degree Harley and 90-degree Ducati, or transverse, as favoured by Moto Guzzi.

Three-cylinder engines can be arranged either across the frame, as with Triumphs and Laverdas, or along the line of the bike like BMW's K75. Likewise with in-line fours, where BMW's K series follows the old Henderson/ Indian longitudinal layout, but with horizontal instead of vertical cylinders. Many modern bikes use the familiar Japanese transverse format popularized in 1969 by Honda's CB750.

Honda fours also include the V-four of the VFR750 and the flat-four of the earlier Gold Wing models. Ariel's legendary Square Four was named after its unusual engine layout.

Five-cylinder bikes are rare, the most original being the amazing 1922 Megola,

■ RIGHT *Different approaches to four-stroke valve design are highlighted by pistons from (clockwise from top left): a two-valves-per-cylinder Moto Guzzi; a two-valve Harley-Davidson; a four-valve Suzuki GSX-R; and a five-valve Yamaha FZ750.*

whose 640cc five-pot engine was arranged radially inside the front wheel. The modern 1500cc Gold Wing is a watercooled flat-six; other six-cylinder designs include the straight-six Honda CBX1000, Kawasaki Z1300 and Benelli 750 of the 1970s.

Laverda raced a V6 in 1978, and fellow Italian firm Morbidelli has produced an exotic 850cc V-eight to power a prototype sports-tourer. Meanwhile the mighty Boss Hoss makes do with the V-eight Chevy unit commonly found in American cars.

Anatomy of a Motorcycle

TWO-STROKES AND ROTARIES

Two-stroke motors are lighter and potentially more powerful than four-strokes of similar capacity, which is why they are used for Grand Prix racebikes. They are also mechanically simpler and generally cheaper to produce, which is why they are popular for small commuter bikes. But the two-stroke's workings are more complex. Instead of having mechanical valves, a two-stroke uses the underneath of the piston to force the incoming mixture of fuel and air into the combustion chamber, via the crankcase and connecting transfer ports.

This allows the engine to fire with every rotation of the crankshaft (ie, every two strokes), rather than every two rotations (or four strokes), which gives the "stroker" its power advantage. But it means that lubricating oil cannot sit in the crankcases, and must be carried in the fuel/air mixture and burnt,

■ ABOVE *Suzuki's RG500 features rotary disc valve induction. Its carburettors are mounted on the side of the crankcase, and induction is controlled by slotted discs that spin with the crankshaft.*

■ ABOVE RIGHT *A piston-ported two-stroke such as Yamaha's TZ750 has a non-return reed valve between each carburettor and the engine. This allows mixture in, and prevents it from being blown back.*

adding to pollution. And despite the modern two-stroke tuner's skill in selecting the correctly shaped expansion chamber for the exhaust system, some of the mixture goes down the exhaust without being burnt – further increasing emissions. These problems are being addressed by the new wave of clean two-strokes under development.

■ **TYPES OF TWO-STROKE ENGINE**

Many of the best two-strokes have been parallel twins, from the Scott Squirrel of motorcycling's early years to Yamaha's recent RD350LC. Kawasaki's late 1970s KR250 and 350 Grand Prix racers were tandem twins, with one cylinder behind the other. Modern Grand Prix 250s are in-line V-twins, as are several roadsters including Aprilia's RS250. Two-stroke triples have included 1970s classics such as Kawasaki's aircooled 750cc H2 and 500cc H1, and Suzuki's watercooled GT750.

Freddie Spencer's 1983 world championship winning Honda NS500 was a V-triple, as was the NS400 roadster it subsequently spawned. Four-cylinder two-strokes have included

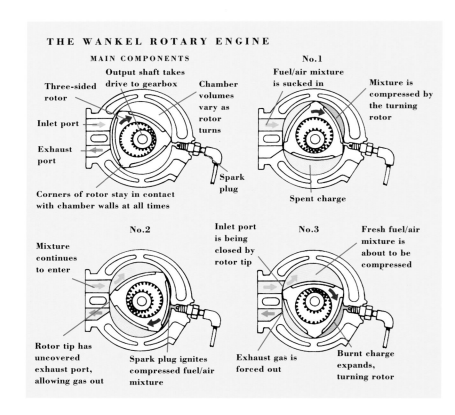

THE WANKEL ROTARY ENGINE

MAIN COMPONENTS

Output shaft takes drive to gearbox

Three-sided rotor

Chamber volumes vary as rotor turns

Inlet port

Exhaust port

Corners of rotor stay in contact with chamber walls at all times

Spark plug

No.1

Fuel/air mixture is sucked in

Mixture is compressed by the turning rotor

Spent charge

No.2

Mixture continues to enter

Inlet port is being closed by rotor tip

Rotor tip has uncovered exhaust port, allowing gas out

Spark plug ignites compressed fuel/air mixture

No.3

Fresh fuel/air mixture is about to be compressed

Exhaust gas is forced out

Burnt charge expands, turning rotor

■ BELOW LEFT *Kawasaki's 750cc H2 aircooled triple of the early 1970s was smelly, thirsty, noisy, inflexible — and very powerful indeed.*

■ BELOW RIGHT *Most two-strokes have followed Suzuki's GT750 triple in using watercooling for a more controlled operating temperature.*

THE TWO-STROKE CYCLE

A INDUCTION
As the piston rises, the fuel/air mixture in the cylinder is compressed, while fresh mixture is being drawn into the crankcase

B TRANSFER
As the piston descends on the power stroke, it first compresses the fuel/air mixture in the crankcase, and then uncovers the transfer port (on right of diagram) through which the mixture is forced into the cylinder

C COMPRESSION
The piston's upward movement compresses the charge in the combustion chamber

D COMBUSTION
As the piston nears the top of its stroke the mixture is ignited, after which the piston begins its downwards, or power, stroke

A INDUCTION

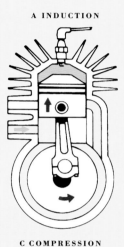

B TRANSFER

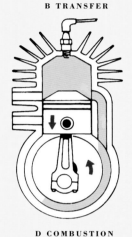

C COMPRESSION

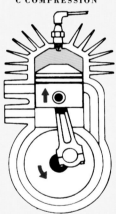

D COMBUSTION

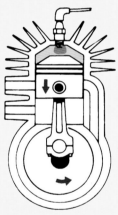

E EXHAUST
Near the bottom of the power stroke, the piston uncovers the exhaust port. The burnt gases escape due to their own pressure and by being displaced by the fresh charge being forced through the transfer port. Despite two-stroke tuners' best efforts, some fresh mixture is inevitably lost through the exhaust port

E EXHAUST

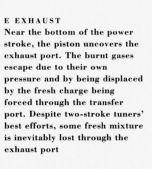

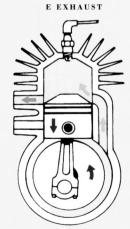

Yamaha's straight-four TZ750 racer and Suzuki's racing and road-going square-four RG500. Recent 500cc Grand Prix racers have been V-fours. Honda's NSR500 has a single crankshaft while Suzuki's and Yamaha's V-fours use two geared-together cranks.

■ THE ROTARY ENGINE

The smoothest engine of all is the Wankel rotary, named after its inventor, Felix Wankel. A figure-of-eight shaped chamber holds a three-sided rotor, which turns in such a way that its corners always remain in contact with the sides. The rotor's movement forms three compartments of varying volume, in which the suck-squeeze-bang-blow cycle takes place. The Wankel engine can be powerful, compact and light although fuel consumption is high. Rotary roadsters from DKW, Suzuki and Norton have not, however, been commercially successful.

■ ABOVE *Norton's Classic roadster proved that a rotary bike engine could be neat, reasonably powerful, and very smooth.*

■ BELOW *Bimota's SB6 uses an ultra-rigid development of the aluminium twin-spar frame layout used by most modern sportsbikes.*

Anatomy of a Motorcycle

FRAMES AND SUPENSION

The motorcycle's basic layout may have changed little during this century but chassis performance has improved hugely – as a ride on most classic bikes, with their heavy, flexible frames and crude suspension, confirms. Handling depends on many variables, notably frame strength and geometry, weight distribution, suspension type and adjustment. All have been affected by advances in chassis technology, leading to modern machines that are stable, well-balanced and comfortable over a wide range of speeds and road conditions.

Until the 1950s, many bikes had thin steel frames and springer front forks with no damping or a simple friction arrangement. Rear suspension was provided by a crude plunger set-up or was non-existent leaving the rider cushioned only by the back tyre and a sprung saddle – not surprisingly this was known as a hard tail. Later models had sturdier frames, either of pressed steel or, in the case of the legendary Norton Featherbed, braced and often triangulated steel tubes designed to hold a pair of hydraulically damped rear shock absorbers. Sometimes, as with Honda's four-cylinder racers of the 1960s, the engine was an integral stressed member of the frame.

The increases in superbike engine's power and weight in the 1970s left many chassis

unable to cope – leading to wobbles and weaves – but technology has moved fast in recent years. A typical modern sportsbike has a rigid frame, particularly in the crucial link between steering head and swing-arm pivot. Frame design may incorporate a traditional tubular steel cradle, a large diameter main spine as used by Triumph, a space-frame or ladder of thinner tubes – a recognizable Ducati trademark – or the common sports and racing format of twin aluminium spars.

■ **SUSPENSION DESIGN**

Front forks and rear shock units work in essentially the same way. They absorb shocks with a coil spring, using a hydraulic damper – oil forced through holes of various sizes – to control the rate of its compression (bump or compression damping) and, more importantly, of its return (rebound damping). Suspension action produces heat, so many modern shock units have remote oil reservoirs, situated alongside or away from the main unit, to aid cooling.

The more sophisticated front and rear units are adjustable, both for spring preload – which controls the amount of weight needed to

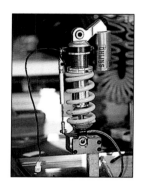

■ ABOVE *At the Öhlins factory in Sweden, shock units are developed and tested with the aid of sophisticated suspension dynamometers.*

■ LEFT *Many modern Harleys use hidden suspension units to give the look of a genuine hard-tail such as the 1949 model WL45.*

■ LEFT *The sales
failure of Yamaha's
stable-handling
GTS1000 was a setback
to development of
alternative front
suspension systems.*

compress the unit further – and for
compression and rebound damping. Multiple
springs of different rates can be used to give a
progressive effect. At the rear, rising rate
suspension is more commonly provided by a
mechanical linkage system at one end of the
shock. This allows a light action for small
bumps, and a firmer response nearer the end of
the spring's travel to prevent bottoming out.

■ **ALTERNATIVE FRONT
SUSPENSION**

Many engineers argue that telescopic forks are
a poor solution – because they are affected by
braking, and acted upon by forces in directions
they are not designed for. Alternative hub-
centre designs, in which the front wheel pivots
on a bearing inside its hub, get over these problems and separate the processes of steering
and braking. Bimota's Tesi and Yamaha's
GTS1000 use different forkless systems to
provide a high degree of stability, particularly
under braking. But neither has proved
commercially successful, partly because of
high costs but mostly because modern front
forks actually work very well indeed.

■ **CHASSIS GEOMETRY**

The way a bike handles is greatly affected by
the geometry of its chassis. A modern racebike
has a short wheelbase, steep front forks, very

little trail and plenty of weight over its front
wheel for quick and light steering – often at the
expense of marginal stability.

At the other extreme, a cruiser is set up for
stability, with raked forks, lots of trail, a long
wheelbase and more weight over the rear
wheel. Most roadsters fall somewhere in-
between, and some chassis can be fine-tuned
using adjustable fork yokes to vary rake and
trail, plus various methods to raise or lower the
front or rear suspension.

■ RIGHT *Bimota's
Yamaha-engined YB4
and YB6 were among
the first sportsbikes to
use the now-common
alloy beam frame
format.*

■ BELOW *Triumph's
modular chassis is
based around a large-
diameter steel spine
frame, with the engine
used as a stressed
member.*

Anatomy of a Motorcycle

WHEELS, TYRES AND BRAKES

The motorcycle's inherent instability makes its tyres and brakes all the more important, especially as the need to lean in corners means that even the biggest and most powerful bikes have tyres whose footprint is precariously narrow by car standards. Until the 1960s most bikes wore tubed front and rear tyres of crossply construction and roughly similar size. In contrast, modern sports machines achieve incredible cornering angles – well in excess of 45 degrees – due largely to the high levels of grip provided by their sticky, low-profile, tubeless radial tyres, the rear of which is much wider than the front to cope with high levels of power. Soft-compound superbike rear tyres are often worn out after less than 2000 miles (3218 kilometres) of hard road use.

Increasingly specialized demand has led to an extraordinary variety of tyre types, from treadless racing slicks designed to put down maximum surface area in dry conditions, but useless in the wet, to heavily treaded knobbly tyres for trials or motocross events. In-between come sports tyres which are lightly treaded (because tread flex increases heat build-up, thus reducing performance) and harder, more comprehensively patterned tyres for commuting or touring. Dual-purpose tyres, designed for trail bikes, are generally biased towards road riding and of limited use in heavy mud. Road-racing wet tyres, with block-pattern tread and ultra-soft compound, can wear out literally in minutes if used on a dry track.

The most notable advance in motorbike wheels has been the move from wire-spoked to cast-construction, something which happened gradually through the 1970s and 1980s. Cast wheels, normally made of aluminium but sometimes of lighter magnesium, are generally stronger and can accept modern tubeless tyres.

■ LEFT *This shows only part of the huge collection of wheels and tyres that Yamaha's 500cc Grand Prix team requires for each race.*

■ BELOW *The Manx Norton's combination of Roadholder forks, wire front wheel and twin-leading-shoe brake was impressive in the l960s.*

■ BELOW *A front disc brake with single-piston caliper was a very sophisticated feature when Honda's CB750 four was released in l969.*

■ BELOW *This Suzuki RGV500 racer is fitted with upside-down forks and huge carbon-fibre brake discs, gripped by four-piston calipers.*

■ BELOW *The rear end of Ducati's 916 features a single-sided swing arm and an ultra-wide, 190-section radial tyre for maximum roadholding.*

■ BELOW *BMW's single-shock R1100GS trail bike uses a system of rods to counter its shaft-drive motor's effect on handling.*

Wire wheels, however, are still fitted to some new bikes, mainly to emphasize their retro look. Sportsbike wheel diameter has become standardized at 17 inches front and rear, although notable exceptions include Honda's CBR900RR, which uses a 16-inch front. In the early 1980s the fashion was for 16-inch front wheels – led, as with much in roadster chassis design, by developments in Grand Prix racing.

■ BRAKE DESIGN

Until fairly recently most motorbikes were stopped by drum brakes, and some small bikes still are. This consists of a pair of semi-circular shoes which are forced open against the inside of the drum when the brake is applied. Some drums, such as those fitted to the otherwise magnificent Brough Superior, were notably poor, and prone to overheating and fading with hard use. Others, such as the big, ventilated four-leading-shoe Grimecas used by specials and racebikes in the 1960s, were very powerful although they required regular adjustment to give optimum performance.

Disc brakes began to take over the motorcycle world in the early 1970s, led by Honda's CB750. A simple system consists of a single steel disc gripped by the twin pads of a hydraulically operated caliper. Discs don't

require adjustment for wear and tend to cope better with the heat generated by braking, but early systems worked very poorly in wet weather. Modern superbikes use twin front discs, with another at the rear, gripped by calipers each containing four or even six individual pistons for improved power and feel. Some bikes, including several Moto Guzzis and Honda's CBR1000F, use hydraulics to link front and rear brakes.

Several manufacturers have developed efficient anti-lock or ABS systems, but the complexity and expense is such that fitment is restricted to BMWs and sports-tourers such as Honda's ST1100 and Yamaha's GTS1000.

■ BELOW *This Michelin rack in a roadrace paddock holds (from left) two front slicks; a wider rear slick; heavily treaded rear and front wets; a lightly treaded front intermediate; and two more front slicks.*

Sport on Two Wheels

The Olympic motto, *citius, altius, fortius*, meaning faster, higher, stronger can equally be applied to competition aboard motorcycles.

Almost as long as bikes have been built, people have been holding contests to see who could make them go quickest, last longest — even get to the top of the biggest hill.

Motorcycle competition does not have to be all about speed. The sport of trials, for example, produces champions as skilful as any on two wheels. Endurance often plays a part, whether in a 24-hour road-race or the three-week slog from Paris to Dakar. But mostly it's the thrill of high velocities that attracts riders and spectators to bike sport. This is true wherever they are in the world, and on whatever surface they compete — from the steep, man-made banking at Daytona to the sand of the Baja desert; from frozen ice-race ovals to the unforgiving public roads of the Isle of Man.

EARLY RACERS

■ OPPOSITE *Top Texan racer Eddie Hasha poses in front of a steeply banked board-track, or motordrome, with Indian's new eight-valve V-twin in 1911. In the following year he and seven others died following a crash at Newark in New Jersey.*

When motorcycle racing began, at the end of the last century, riders had to contend not only with their rivals but with the fragility of their crude bikes and the often appalling condition of the roads. Many early racing machines were tricycles, some with engines as large as two litres. Riders competed in gruelling inter-city marathons on temperamental bikes with no suspension, typically wearing clothing no more protective than a woolly jumper, plus-fours, stout shoes and a peaked cap.

Continental Europe was the birthplace not just of the motorcycle but also of bike racing, with the first major event being held between Paris and Rouen in July 1894. The next year saw pioneering races in both Italy and America. Other, even longer, events around the turn of the century included Paris-Vienna and

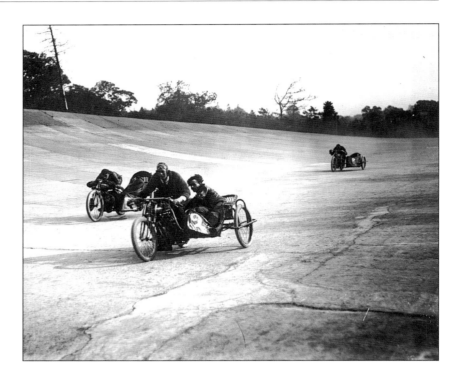

■ ABOVE *The width and banking of the concrete Brooklands track are clear in this shot of a Zenith outfit leading a race "for cycles and sidecars" in 1913.*

■ LEFT *The stopwatch is running as Sunbeam rider HR Davies gets under way at Caerphilly in Wales on a hill-climb, a popular early form of competition.*

■ RIGHT *Flying Merkel factory racer Maldwyn Jones won second place in a 300-mile (480 kilometre) race, at Savannah, Georgia in 1913.*

■ BELOW *These Indian V-twins hit 100mph (160 kph) with no suspension or brakes, and tyres prone to coming off the rims.*

Paris-Madrid. In the early 1900s short-circuit races became popular, often held on banked cycle tracks such as those at Lille and Paris's *Parc des Princes* in France, and at Plymouth and Crystal Palace in Britain.

The first big international race took place in France in 1904. The Coupe International was a 170-mile (273-kilometre) event in which a maximum of three bikes from each country was allowed. French rider Demester won on a Griffon, at an average speed of 45.1mph (72.5kph), but the race was declared void due to the dubious legality of the winning bikes, and after it became clear that tyres had been sabotaged by nails sprinkled by spectators.

The year 1907 was notable for two momentous events in Britain, one of which was the first-ever Tourist Trophy meeting in the Isle of Man. The other was the opening of Brooklands, the world's first artificially constructed race circuit. Surfaced with concrete and 2.8 miles (4.5 kilometres) in length, the egg-shaped Surrey track included two high and wide banked turns, remains of which are still visible today. Brooklands' layout allowed high speeds and attracted bike racers, record-breakers and testers until its closure at the start of the Second World War.

■ ABOVE RIGHT *Rem Fowler overcame mechanical problems to win the twin-cylinder class of the first TT in 1907 on this Peugeot-engined Norton.*

■ BELOW *Three competitors get under way side-by-side in this 1913 shot of the Brighton Speed Trials, an event that still takes place today.*

Banked tracks of a different kind became popular in America, where big V-twins from Indian, Thor and Flying Merkel thundered round narrow wooden circuits with sides as steep as 60 degrees. These were thrilling and highly dangerous events, at which professional racers with names like "Fearless" Balke and "Dare Devil" Derkum raced head-to-head, reaching speeds of 100mph (160kph), in front of crowds of 10,000 people. Board-racing's decline can be traced almost exactly to the day when two riders and six spectators were killed in a crash at Newark, New Jersey in 1912.

RACING ON THE ROADS

For many years the Isle of Man Tourist Trophy was the world's greatest motorcycle racing event. Even today there are those who maintain that the legendary 37.7-mile (60.6-kilometre) Mountain course makes the TT the supreme test of rider and machine. And although purpose-built circuits now dominate the sport from amateur to world championship level, pure road racing continues at places as far apart as Ireland, Belgium and New Zealand.

The TT's history dates back to 1907, when the Isle of Man was chosen as a race venue because competing on public roads was banned on mainland Britain. The event was known as the Tourist Trophy because machines had to be fitted with brakes, mudguards and a toolbox. Rem Fowler averaged just 36.2mph (58.2kph) when he won the twin-cylinder class on a Peugeot-engined Norton, pedalling up hills and stopping several times to repair punctures and broken drive-belts.

By the early 1920s, winning riders were averaging over 50mph (80kph) in gruelling

■ RIGHT *Charlie Collier, who ran the Matchless firm with his father and brother, won the single-cylinder class of the first TT in 1907, and won again three years later.*

■ BELOW *Mike Hailwood crashed his MV Agusta in the 1965 Senior TT, but got back on again to win with a bleeding nose, a broken fairing and flattened exhaust megaphones.*

races of five or more laps. On his TT debut in 1922, Stanley Woods had time to have his clothes catch fire while refuelling, stop to mend his engine and then crash and remount – yet still finish fifth. Woods went on to win a total of ten TTs between 1923 and 1939. Speeds had risen sharply by 1950, when Norton's Geoff Duke raised the lap record to 93.33mph (150.19kph) on the way to his first victory. Duke dominated the TT during the 1950s with six wins, but it was Bob McIntyre who set the first 100mph (160kph) lap – riding a four-cylinder Gilera in 1957.

Heroes in the 1960s included Giacomo Agostini, who scored ten wins, and Mike Hailwood, whose total of 14 victories included the 1967 Senior in which ";Mike the Bike" beat "Ago" in the race that many fans still consider to be the greatest TT of all time.

Hailwood's most famous win came in 1978 when he returned from retirement to take the Formula One race on a Ducati. By then the TT had lost its world championship status, and

■ BELOW *Hailwood returned from retirement to ride a Ducati to an emotional Formula One TT win in 1978.*

■ RIGHT *Joey Dunlop's exploits at the TT and his native Ireland earned him the title "King of the Roads".*

■ BELOW *The beauty and danger of the TT circuit are clear as Scottish star Steve Hislop ignores the speed limit on the exit of Ginger Hall.*

stars such as Barry Sheene and Kenny Roberts refused to risk the obvious dangers of racing at speed between stone walls.

But the TT continued to produce its own breed of heroes into the 1990s, when men like Joey Dunlop — who won a record nineteenth

TT in 1995 — and Steve Hislop lapped at average speeds of 120mph (193kph). Racing on the roads will never regain its former prestige, but events continue to take place at circuits including the TT, Ireland's North West 200 and Belgium's Chimay.

GRAND PRIX 500S

Grand Prix racing's 500cc class is the most prestigious in motorcycling. In the modern era, whoever has worn the 500cc crown has been entitled to call himself the best motorcycle racer in the world. As the most powerful and fastest bikes, the 500s have generally attracted the top riders, the biggest budgets, the greatest interest and the most publicity.

Modern 500 stars battle in a true world championship that in recent years has included rounds as far apart as Australia, America and Argentina. The situation was very different in 1949, when the world championship was first formed from the "Continental Circus" — the band of riders who, with their bikes and a few spares in small vans, followed a winding route around Europe from one race to the next. Britain's Les Graham won the 500cc title after six rounds, all of which were in Europe.

Graham won that first 500cc crown on a British twin, the AJS Porcupine, and Geoff Duke took the championship two years later on a single-cylinder Norton. But for the rest of the

■ RIGHT *John Surtees began MV Agusta's domination of the 500cc world championship in 1956, with the first of his four titles for the Italian factory.*

■ BELOW *The AJS Porcupine was originally designed for supercharging, but in "unblown" form took Les Graham to the first 500cc title in 1949.*

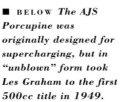

1950s, 1960s and early 1970s, racing's premier class was dominated by multi-cylinder Italian four-strokes, firstly from Gilera — whose six championships included a hat-trick from Duke between 1953 and 1955 — and then from MV Agusta.

MV's red and silver machines set records that will probably never be equalled, winning 17 consecutive world 500cc championships between 1958 and 1974 as well as a total of 38 riders' world titles and 37 manufacturers' championships. The so-called "Gallarate Fire Engines" reigned supreme in the 500cc class, winning the championship with John Surtees in 1956 and then, after a year's break, regaining it with Surtees, Gary Hocking and Mike Hailwood, who won four in a row.

Competition between numerous Italian factories was intense until the mid-1950s. But

■ BELOW *Giacomo Agostini's haul of eight 500cc and seven 350cc world championships makes him the most successful Grand Prix rider of all.*

■ LEFT *Gilera's DOHC four changed the face of 500cc Grand Prix racing, winning six titles and providing the inspiration for MV Agusta's similar machines.*

■ BELOW *Guzzi withdrew from Grands Prix before the legendary 500cc V-eight, pictured in the factory museum, could prove its worth.*

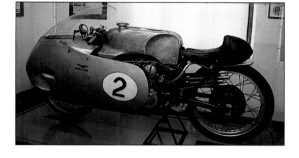

■ BELOW *The changing face of 500cc racing is summed-up in this 1975 shot of Barry Sheene, on a two-stroke Suzuki, coming up behind reigning world champion Phil Read riding the four-stroke MV Agusta.*

Mondial, Moto Guzzi and Gilera quit the arena in 1957, Guzzi without ever realizing the full potential of their exotic and super-fast V-eight. MV's next serious works challenge came from Mike Hailwood who left for Honda in 1966 and twice came desperately close to taking the title, with Agostini just beating him each time. Honda then quit racing, and Ago went on to take seven consecutive championships for MV.

Phil Read retained the 500cc title for MV in 1973 and 1974 but the Japanese two-stroke challenge was looming. Ironically though, it was Italian hero, Agostini, who in 1975 won the title for Yamaha, ending Agusta's glory years and confirming the two-stroke as the dominant force in 500cc Grand Prix racing.

GP 500s: The Two-stroke Era

Modern 500cc Grand Prix bikes are the purest, most highly developed motorbikes on the planet. On the straights their 185bhp two-stroke engines produce top speeds of up to 200mph (322kph). In the corners their light weight, ultra-rigid frames, sophisticated suspension and fat slick tyres allow incredible angles of lean. The factory 500s' performance is so violent and demanding that only a select band of talented and highly-paid professionals – men like past champions Eddie Lawson, Wayne Gardner, Wayne Rainey, Kevin Schwantz and Michael Doohan – can even come near to mastering them.

■ LEFT *Factory honour is at stake as Shinichi Itoh (Honda, 7), Alexandre Barros (Suzuki, 6), Daryl Beattie (Yamaha, 3) and Doug Chandler (Cagiva, 10) battle in the 1994 Italian Grand Prix.*

■ BELOW *Kevin Schwantz, world champion in 1993, retired two years later after a Grand Prix career that contained many victories and almost as many injuries.*

The two-stroke revolution began with Yamaha who, in the early 1970s, first built a 500cc four: basically two twins combined, with the cylinders set in line across the frame. With

■ LEFT *Honda's Freddie Spencer and Yamaha's Kenny Roberts, here at the Italian Grand Prix, clashed many times during the 1983 season.*

■ BELOW *The Suzuki RG500s of Barry Sheene and Dutch star Wil Hartog lead Kenny Roberts' Yamaha in the French Grand Prix at Nogaro in 1978.*

■ ABOVE *Freddie Spencer won two 500cc titles in the 1980s.*

■ BELOW *Australian ace Michael Doohan retained the champion's No.1 plate in 1995.*

double the number of power strokes for a given engine speed, a two-stroke should always produce more power than an equivalent capacity four-stroke, and Yamaha's format was immediately a major success. Jarno Saarinen won the French Grand Prix on the four's debut in 1973. Although the Finnish star was killed later that year, Yamaha's Giacomo Agostini went on to win the Daytona 200 in 1974 and the 500cc world title the following season.

Suzuki's more compact square-four RG500 took Barry Sheene to the championship in 1976 and 1977. Kenny Roberts then arrived on the scene to win three consecutive titles on his straight-four YZR Yamaha, redefining the art of riding a 500cc Grand Prix bike with a

power-sliding style developed from American dirt-track racing. Suzuki and the RG hit back, with championships for Italians Marco Lucchinelli and Franco Uncini, before Freddie Spencer finally won Honda's first 500cc title in 1983 on the NS500 two-stroke triple.

Since then, the dominant 500cc engine layout has been the V-four, with Honda's NSR, Yamaha's YZR and Suzuki's RGV each taking championships in recent years, and Cagiva's V-four becoming competitive before the Italian firm's withdrawal from Grand Prix racing at the end of 1994.

The future of Grand Prix racing was then unclear, although in many ways the 500cc class had never been healthier. Teams had become increasingly professional, worldwide television coverage had brought the sport to millions, grids were full and tracks had been made safer than ever before. Serious accidents, like the one that left triple-champion Wayne Rainey paralysed in 1993, are a sad and inevitable fact of motorcycle racing. But it was not such events that threatened the health of Grand Prix racing. The exotic, hugely expensive 500s were under threat from the road-based Superbikes that were regarded by some manufacturers as more relevant to motorcycle sales.

■ BELOW *Phil Read keeps his two-stroke Yamaha twin ahead of Jim Redman's Honda four-stroke twin in a 350cc race at Mallory Park in 1964.*

THE SMALLER GP CLASSES

The smaller Grand Prix categories can't match the straight-line speed or the sheer glamour of the 500s – but they often more than make up for that with closer racing, more technical variety and a wider number of potential winners. The thrilling sight of six or more tiny 125s and riders slipstreaming each other down the straights and clashing fairings through bends for lap after lap has long been commonplace. In countries such as Spain, riders of the tiddlers, diminutive giants such as Angel Nieto and Jorge "Aspar" Martinez have traditionally been regarded as highly as big-bike champions.

In recent seasons, racing's rules have limited Grand Prix 125s to a single cylinder and 250s to two, with six gears apiece. But rules were less restrictive in the past, which inspired some remarkable bikes. The Suzuki RK66 on which Hans-Georg Anscheidt won the 50cc

world title in 1966, for example, had two cylinders, 14 gears and made 17.5bhp at 17,300rpm. Honda and MV Agusta built many multi-cylinder 250s and 350s in the 1960s. In 1964 the Japanese factory unveiled the

■ BELOW *Haruchika Aoki (No.12), one of several outstanding Japanese 125cc riders, screams his Honda into the lead in the 1995 Spanish Grand Prix.*

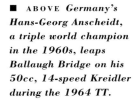

■ ABOVE *Germany's Hans-Georg Anscheidt, a triple world champion in the 1960s, leaps Ballaugh Bridge on his 50cc, 14-speed Kreidler during the 1964 TT.*

legendary 250cc, six-cylinder RC166, which reached 150mph (241kph). The next season Honda's Luigi Taveri won the 125cc title on an exotic five-cylinder machine.

In recent years the Grand Prix solo classes have comprised just 500s, 250s and 125s, but in the past there have also been races for 350 and 50 or 80cc bikes. Riders commonly used to contest more than one class. In 1967 Mike Hailwood rode works Hondas in the 250, 350 and 500cc classes. At Assen, after winning his

third Dutch TT of the day, Hailwood almost fell off his motorcycle through sheer exhaustion. Riders often contested both 250 and 350cc championships until the larger class was dropped in 1983, and both Kork Ballington and Anton Mang scored double championship wins aboard Kawasaki's tandem twins.

One of racing's most spectacular achievements was Freddie Spencer's 250 and 500cc championship double for Honda in 1985. Since then the increasingly competitive nature of Grand Prix racing, together with the contrasting technique required to get the best from the 250cc twins and the almost doubly powerful 500cc V-fours, has kept riders to one class. High cornering speed has always been crucial on 125s and 250s, while the ultra-powerful 500s demanded the "slow in, fast out" style refined by Kenny Roberts. Even 250cc champions such as Christian Sarron and Sito Pons struggled to repeat their success after moving up to 500s, although evolving engine and tyre technology have made the transition slightly smoother in recent seasons.

SIDECAR RACING

Racing sidecars are very different vehicles
from the road-going motorcycle combinations
to which they are related. Far from being a
bike with a sidecar alongside, a modern racing
outfit is a specialized structure whose
aluminium one-piece chassis holds three
small-diameter wheels, each wearing a fat,
square-section tyre. These machines have more
in common with a racing car than with a bike.

It was not always this way. When sidecar
racing first became popular in the 1920s,
outfits were indeed solos with a lightweight,

large-wheeled chair bolted on. In 1923 the first
Isle of Man sidecar TT was won by Freddie
Dixon, whose Douglas outfit featured a lever
with which passenger Walter Perry made the
machine bank through corners. Banking
Flxicar sidecars were also successful in
American dirt-track racing in the 1920s. By
the time Britain's Eric Oliver won the first of
his four sidecar world championships in 1949,
the sidecar had become much lower so
allowing the passenger, Denis Jenkinson, to
lean out in left-hand bends.

■ ABOVE *Alain Michel's passenger had no time for the view as their LCR outfit sped up the Mistral straight at Circuit Paul Ricard.*

■ BELOW *Owen Greenwood's Mini (No.7), ahead of world champion Scheidegger in this 1966 shot from Mallory Park.*

Switzerland and Germany have produced many of the world's best sidecar drivers and designers over the years. Germany's Max Deubel and Emil Horner won four consecutive championships on BMW flat-twins in the 1960s. Swiss Fritz Scheidegger won two titles and did much to advance technical thinking in sidecars. German Helmut Fath won the championship in 1960 with a BMW, and returned after a serious injury to win it again

eight years later with the URS, whose four-cylinder four-stroke engine he built himself.

Two-strokes took over in the 1970s, initially with German Königs and then with Yamahas. The sidecar's chassis revolution came a few years later, led by the Swiss Seymaz, whose monocoque aluminium platform and car-style suspension and wheels gave a lower, lighter machine than the traditional steel frame and telescopic forks. The 1980s and early 1990s were dominated by the LCR chassis, designed by Swiss Louis Christen and a development of the theme.

The greatest driver of modern times is Switzerland's Rolf Biland, who in 1994 won a record seventh championship. Biland also helped develop the BRM V-four engine, which proved powerful but unreliable in 1995, and was intended for use in both sidecars and 500cc solos. But in other respects the gap between two and three-wheeled racing has widened. Although sidecars retain a following they have been excluded from many Grand Prix venues, and their future remains in doubt.

SUPERBIKES

Superbikes are the rising force of bike racing. Visually similar to, and directly derived from, road-going machines, the big four-strokes are strictly limited in the modifications allowed. That often makes for close racing. In recent seasons, booming Ducati V-twins and screaming four-cylinder Japanese 750s, backed by the major factories and ridden by top riders such as Scott Russell and Carl Fogarty, have provided some memorable racing battles.

Superbike racing began in America, where the tradition of competing on modified streetbikes dates back to the 1970s. Then riders such as Reg Pridmore, Wes Cooley and Steve McLaughlin locked high handlebars on BMW flat-twins and 1000cc fours from Suzuki and Kawasaki. In the early 1980s, rising stars Freddie Spencer (Honda) and Eddie Lawson (Kawasaki) clashed on big four-strokes before

moving into Grands Prix. Fellow future 500cc world champions Wayne Rainey and Kevin Schwantz also raced and won on superbikes. But in those days the class was a poor relation; the bikes disparagingly referred to as diesels by Grand Prix riders.

That attitude began to change in 1988, when the World Superbike Championship was established by McLaughlin, the former rider who earlier had been instrumental in starting the US series. Another flamboyant American,

■ ABOVE *The Ducatis of Carl Fogarty, champion Doug Polen and Frenchman Raymond Roche emphasize the Italian factory's Superbike strength at Donington Park in 1992.*

■ LEFT *Californian Fred Merkel, riding for an Italian-based team, won the first World Superbike championship on an RC30 fitted with factory race-kit parts.*

■ LEFT *In 1994 Carl Fogarty fought a season-long battle with Kawasaki's reigning champion Scott Russell (No.1) before recapturing the title for Ducati.*

■ BELOW *Freddie Spencer, pictured at Daytona, 1980, rode a four-cylinder Honda Superbike before graduating to Grands Prix.*

■ BOTTOM *Steve McLaughlin won American national Superbike races on a Suzuki GS1000 in the late 1970s.*

"Flyin' Fred" Merkel, won the first two titles on a factory-backed Honda RC30, and the roadster-based series was an immediate success. Italy's Ducati then took over – aided by rules allowing twins a capacity and weight advantage over fours – with championship victories for Frenchman Raymond Roche in 1990 and America's Doug Polen in 1991 and 1992.

The subsequent sales success of Ducati's red race-replica V-twins highlighted the commercial potential to be gained from Superbike success, and the factories stepped up their involvement. Scott Russell won on a lime-green works Kawasaki ZXR750 before Carl Fogarty regained the crown for Ducati in 1994. Honda joined in again, initially unsuccessfully, with the V-four RC45.

By 1995 Yamaha had boosted its presence with a full works team, and Bimota had also joined the fray. Suzuki, Aprilia and Cagiva – the latter having quit Grands Prix in favour of Superbikes – waited in the wings.

Superbike racing's high level of competition, relatively low cost and big influence on roadster sales had raised the possibility, unthinkable just a few years earlier, that the four-stroke class would replace Grands Prix as bike racing's star attraction.

ENDURANCE RACING

Long-distance racing adds an extra dimension to the spectacle of high-speed motorcycling. Modern endurance events are run at a furious pace, and races of up to 24 hours contain fuel-stops, rider and tyre changes – all conducted in just a few seconds – and hours of hard riding through the night. For riders who crash or break down, the race can include a long push back to the pits, after which a team of well-drilled mechanics works flat-out to get a damaged bike back onto the track.

Things were less hectic but even more tiring when the Bol d'Or, the oldest and most famous 24-hour event, was first held on the outskirts of Paris in 1922. The winning rider – only one

was allowed per machine – covered over 750 miles (1206 kilometres) on a 500cc Motosacoche. By 1930 the Bol, held on a different road circuit near Paris, was attracting over 50,000 spectators and had become an important showcase for manufacturers. Best and toughest of the early racers was Gustave Lefèvre, who had five solo wins on a 500cc Norton, and then two more after co-riders were allowed in 1954.

In the 1970s endurance became a demanding proving ground for large-capacity roadsters. BSA/Triumph triples won in 1970 and 1971, before big four-cylinder Hondas and Kawasakis took over. Bikes raced by legendary

■ BELOW *Riders run across the track to their bikes in the traditional Le Mans start, with fastest qualifiers on the left, as the famous 24-hour race gets under way at the French circuit in 1987.*

■ LEFT *The pit lane stays busy at night during the Spa 24-hour race in Belgium, as lap-scorers signal times to riders, and bikes arrive for refuelling or repair.*

■ RIGHT *French endurance ace Jean-Claude Chemarin won races for both Honda and Kawasaki, on whose 1000cc four he is pictured at the Bol d'Or in 1983.*

■ FAR RIGHT *Honda's factory 750cc V-four RVF dominated endurance racing in the mid-1980s, and formed the basis of the Japanese firm's RC30 roadster.*

■ RIGHT *Works endurance bikes can be refuelled and given fresh tyres in just a few seconds, and every moment can be vital — as Kawasaki's Scott Russell discovered when he lost the 1994 Suzuka eight-hour race to Honda by less than a third of a second.*

French pairings such as Godier/Genoud and Chemarin/Léon housed factory-tuned 1000cc motors in specially built chassis. Many innovative engineering solutions were tried and endurance trends were often copied on road-going superbikes.

In more recent years three riders have been allowed in 24-hour races, and bikes have been limited first to 750cc and then to Superbike format, reducing cost but also outlawing the technically interesting prototypes. Although endurance is unpopular in many countries, and has often failed to support a full-scale world championship, the French 24-hour classics at Le Mans and the Bol d'Or feature top-level factory teams and are unbeatable for atmosphere and drama. The Suzuka eight-hour in Japan, which regularly attracts over 100,000 spectators, is regarded by the Japanese factories as the year's most important race.

MOTOCROSS

Today, a top-level off-road race is almost as likely to take place in a covered arena as in its natural habitat of a dusty, sandy or muddy outdoor track. The old sport of scrambling has developed into motocross and its descendent, supercross, which sees colourfully clad riders – astride tall, lightweight 125 or 250cc single-cylinder two-strokes with long-travel suspension and knobbly tyres – fly over gravity-defying jumps on courses constructed in city stadia.

The link to racing a motorbike around a field remains, but the sport has seen more than the odd change of name since the first off-road meeting was organized in 1924. In that year, a group of riders from Surrey decided to run an adaptation of Yorkshire's Scott trial, excluding the observed sections where points could be lost. Without these the event couldn't be called a trial, and one competitor's comment that the race would be a fair old scramble led to the new form of racing being called scrambling.

Scrambling's popularity spread from Britain to continental Europe in the 1940s, and in 1947 the first international Moto-Cross des Nations was contested between five-man teams from France, Belgium, the Netherlands and England. In the 1960s and 1970s the sport was dominated by Belgian and Scandinavian riders including Joël Robert, Roger De Coster and Heikki Mikkola.

The sport had become known as motocross but was otherwise essentially little changed when it reached America in the late 1960s. Americans had

■ ABOVE *Kurt Nicholl, leading Grand Prix star and British multiple motocross champion, takes a jump in typically effortless style on his factory Honda.*

■ LEFT *Greg Albertyn's 1994 world championship-winning Suzuki RM250 shows off the massive suspension travel it requires for landing from high jumps.*

■ RIGHT *Three-times former world champion Dave Thorpe kicks up the sand as he uses a berm, or bank, to get round a left-hand turn at maximum speed.*

other ideas, and in 1972 the Olympic Coliseum in Los Angeles was converted into an indoor motocross circuit with dramatic jumps.

Supercross had been born, and four years later it had grown into an eight-round national championship, was attracting huge crowds and was on the way to taking over as the most important branch of the sport in the States.

In the last two decades America has produced many spectacular riders including Bob Hannah, Rick Johnson and the most recent superstar, Jeremy McGrath. Americans have proved they can ride outdoors, too, winning every Motocross des Nations from 1981 to 1993. Meanwhile, supercross has in turn been adopted by countries as far apart as Scandinavia, Japan and France. Indoor races at venues such as Bercy in Paris provide an extravaganza of laser-shows, fireworks, huge leaps and wheel-to-wheel racing action.

■ LEFT *The French sport of supermoto, a combination of motocross and road-racing, demonstrated by Gilles Salvador at Paris's Circuit Carole.*

■ BELOW *The first turn of a top-level motocross race is no place for the faint-hearted, as a gang of snarling, dust-throwing motorcycles aims for the same piece of land.*

TRIALS, ENDUROS AND DESERT RACING

Trials bikes' light weight and knobbly, low-pressure tyres allow them to navigate terrain that looks impossible for a mountain goat, let alone a motorcycle. These range from sheer rock faces and deep gullies in conventional trials, to artificial hazards such as huge pipes or a series of tables in the increasingly popular indoor events. Riders often stop completely for several seconds and bounce their machines sideways, all without scoring penalty points by putting a foot on the ground or falling.

Modern courses test mainly the skill and balance of the riders within a time limit, but when the sport began after the turn of the century it was the bikes' reliability that was on trial. Among the most famous events is the Scottish Six Days Trial, which dates from 1910 and attracts a large number of riders ranging from club riders to top professionals, although it is not a world championship event. Another famous trial, the Scott, takes place on the Yorkshire Moors and began as a closed event for workers at the nearby Scott factory.

The most famous trials rider in the 1950s and '60s was Sammy Miller, the Irishman who won over 1000 events, including five Scottish Six Days, on bikes including his famous Ariel with its registration GOV132. In the mid-60s

Miller rode for the Spanish firm Bultaco and helped develop the two-stroke 250cc Sherpa that led the move away from four-stroke singles, known as thumpers. Spain has other leading marques in Gas-Gas and Montesa and has produced many outstanding riders, including multiple world champion Jordi Tarrés. Rivals include Honda, and the Italian firms Aprilia and Beta.

■ LEFT *Until the 1960s, trials were dominated by four-strokes such as the 250cc Greeves Anglian on which Bill Wilkinson won the Scottish Six Days Trial in 1969.*

Enduro, a punishing marathon fought out by teams from all over the world.

The other main form of off-road competition is desert racing, of which the best-known event is the legendary Paris-Dakar Rally. Bikes are generally huge, twin-cylinder four-strokes with long-travel suspension, extra fuel in rear pannier tanks and sophisticated computerized navigation equipment. The Paris-Dakar crosses the Sahara Desert and covers thousands of miles in three weeks – barely one rider in three makes it all the way. Other leading desert races include the Pharaohs in Egypt, and the Baja in Mexico.

Several manufacturers produce desert-replica roadbikes, such as Yamaha's Super Ténéré and Honda's Africa Twin, which are particularly popular in Continental Europe.

Enduro competition lies somewhere between motocross and trials, being essentially an off-road race against the clock for street-legal machines with lights. No points are lost for putting a foot down in sections; instead, riders must make sure to arrive at a series of checkpoints within strict time limits. The most prestigious event is the International Six Day

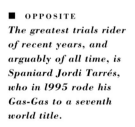

■ OPPOSITE
The greatest trials rider of recent years, and arguably of all time, is Spaniard Jordi Tarrés, who in 1995 rode his Gas-Gas to a seventh world title.

■ RIGHT *Top desert racer Stéphane Peterhansel stands high on the footpegs as he blasts his works Yamaha through the Sahara Desert in the 1994 Paris-Dakar Rally.*

SPEEDWAY, LONG TRACK AND ICE RACING

Speedway bikes have little in common with other motorcycles, being purpose-built for short, four-lap races on quarter-mile (400 metre) dirt ovals. Their engines are 500cc, single-cylinder four-strokes that run on methanol and have just one gear. Their chassis have minimal front suspension and none at the rear, no front brake, and a right footrest set low to take the rider's weight as the bike power-slides through the left-hand bends.

The sport became popular in Australia in the 1920s and took off in Europe after the first British meeting was staged in Essex in 1928. Speedway is essentially a team sport, with meetings consisting of heats between four riders from two rival teams. But the year's biggest event has traditionally been the individual World Final. Sweden's Ove Fundin and New Zealander Barry Briggs each won five

times in the 1950s and 1960s. Ivan Mauger, another New Zealander, won a record sixth title in 1979.

Several other types of racing share speedway's basic format of competing on a tight, anti-clockwise oval. The closest to speedway is long track, a German-dominated sport, also run on shale, whose longer straights

and higher speeds demand engines with two gears. Ivan Mauger won three world titles in the 1970s but the most successful rider is Britain's Simon Wigg, who won his fifth in 1994. Grass-track and sand racing are related but less high-profile sports that require tyre-sliding skills on different surfaces.

The maddest form of bike sport is ice racing on bikes whose tyres bristle with scores of sharp steel spikes. These give excellent grip on the ice, allowing near-horizontal cornering angles, but they can turn a crash into an even nastier experience despite protective wheel-guards that extend part-way around the tyre. Ice racing has generally been dominated by Russians, but is also popular in parts of Eastern Europe and Scandinavia.

Japan has its own brand of speedway called autorace. Held solely to allow the large crowds to bet on the outcome, this takes place on concrete ovals. Eight riders contest each race, on 600cc single or twin-cylinder bikes, which are capable of 120mph (193kph). Prize money levels are high, and leading riders can earn as much as top Grand Prix stars. Nevertheless the temptation to fix results necessitates the imposition of strict rules to ensure that riders are kept away from the crowd before racing.

■ ABOVE *Three battling ice-racers demonstrate the radical cornering angles and aggressive, knee-down styles that are possible despite the slippery track.*

■ LEFT *Ice-race bikes do not slide in bends like speedway machines, but grip the track with long metal spikes fitted to their tyres, which can injure riders in a crash.*

■ BELOW *Speedway's short races and tight tracks combine to make the start particularly important; many races are won by the rider who gets away first.*

DIRT-TRACK AND HILL-CLIMBING

America's most spectacular bike sport takes place on one-mile (1.6-kilometre) ovals, where up to 16 riders thunder round on big Harleys with no front brakes. Through the turns they hold the bikes sideways under power from 100 horsepower V-twin engines, rear tyres throwing up dirt, and on the straights they slipstream or draft at speeds up to 130mph (209kph). The American Motorcycle Association (AMA) Grand National Championship also includes half-mile (800 metre) races, and quarter-mile (400 metre) short tracks, where 600cc single-cylinder bikes are used, and also steeple-chases, which combine elements of dirt-track and motocross.

Dirt-track began on horse tracks at country fairs across America before the First World War. Harley-Davidson's first official race entry was at

■ ABOVE *Jay Spring-steen (No.1) takes his XR750 wide through the "cushion" of loose dirt, while rivals use the firmer "groove" on the inside of the turn.*

the big 300-mile (482-kilometre) event at Dodge City, Kansas, on July 5 1914. The sport was America's most popular in the 1930s but it wasn't until 1946 that the AMA held a one-off championship race at the Springfield Mile, won by Norton-mounted Chet Dykgraff. Harley rider Joe Leonard was the winner in 1954, when the championship was first decided over a series of races, and the American marque has been the most successful ever since.

The most famous dirt-track bike is Harley-Davidson's XR750 V-twin, which was introduced in 1970 and has been taken to victory by dozens of riders, including multiple champion Scott Parker. Honda mounted a successful challenge with the RS750 V-twin, which took four consecutive titles after its introduction in 1984. But the Japanese firm pulled out after the AMA changed the rules to limit the RS's power.

A similar fate met the most outrageous dirt-track bike of all, the four-cylinder, two-stroke Yamaha TZ750 on which Kenny Roberts won the Indianapolis Mile in 1975. Bikes with more than two cylinders were banned at the end of that year and even Roberts didn't complain. The season-long battle for the champion's No.1

■ LEFT *European hill-climbing traditionally takes place on steep and twisty tarmac courses, often with spectacular backdrops such as this one in Devon, England.*

■ BELOW *Harley's in-line V-twin has been dirt-track's dominant engine for years partly due to its controllable power delivery.*

■ OPPOSITE *Scott Stump's left hand is tucked in to improve his XR750's aerodynamics as he enters a straight at the Sacramento Mile, one of the fastest dirt-track venues.*

plate included road races as well as dirt-tracks until separate series were set-up in 1986. Racing dirt-track from a young age has contributed to the road-racing success of many American riders including Roberts, Eddie Lawson and Wayne Rainey.

The other peculiarly American sport is that of hill-climbing – basically a test to see which

rider can go furthest and fastest up a dirt-covered slope that starts steep and gets steeper. Hill-climbing has a long tradition at events such as the famous Widowmaker, and produces long bikes with heavily-treaded rear tyres. An event called hill-climbing also takes place in Europe but this contest is based on timed sprints up a short, twisty tarmac course.

■ ABOVE *Ricky Graham, Bubba Shobert and others were successful on the RS750 before Honda quit after a rule-change made the V-twin less competitive.*

■ RIGHT *Kenny Roberts won the Indianapolis Mile on the TZ750 two-stroke, but still supported its ban.*

DRAG RACING

The quickest and most violent form of bike competition is drag racing — a straight duel of acceleration over a standing-start quarter-mile (0.4-kilometre). The fastest top fuel dragsters produce almost 1000bhp and reach over 220mph (354kph) in just 6.5 seconds — roughly the time a top sports car takes to reach 60mph (96kph). To keep the front wheel down and deliver maximum traction, drag bikes are built long and low, with massively wide rear tyres, and often using wheelie bars that extend far beyond the back of the machine.

Drag racing began in America, where most of the fastest times are still set, although the sport is popular in Europe and elsewhere too. In the early days, Indian and Harley V-twins raced against lighter Triumphs. Japanese motors took

over in the 1970s, when Californian Russ Collins built double and even triple-engined monsters using 750cc Honda power. Another star of the 1970s was Dutchman Henk Vink, known as the "Big Spender", who won many races on a 400bhp twin-engined Kawasaki. The extreme stresses that top fuel engines are exposed to make blow-ups frequent and big budgets essential.

Top fuel bikes have been limited to a single engine since the 1980s, but speeds have increased and in recent years riders have posted times below 6.5 seconds.

Harley-engined dragsters are also now faster than ever — and are often enlarged to over two litres, supercharged and fuelled by nitromethane. The Harley class has increased

■ ABOVE *Instant reactions are vital when the lights change.*

■ BELOW *Terry Vance takes his place on the start-line on one of the ultra-quick Suzukis with which he had much success in the 1980s.*

■ LEFT *Dutchman Henk Vink was Europe's best-known drag-racer of the 1970s, with his consistently spectacular performances on powerful Kawasakis.*

■ BELOW *Under its bodywork the Vance & Hines dragster's motor is based on a 16-valve Suzuki GSX four, but very few original components remain.*

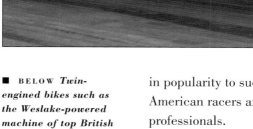

■ BELOW *Twin-engined bikes such as the Weslake-powered machine of top British rider John Hobbs dominated drag racing in the 1970s, but are no longer permitted.*

in popularity to such an extent that some American racers are well-sponsored professionals.

Modern drag meets include numerous classes such as Funny Bike, for machines with roadster-based looks and power aids such as turbochargers or nitrous oxide, and Pro Stock, for highly tuned, near-standard-looking bikes that run on petrol. The cheapest and most basic class is one which allows riders to race on almost any motorcycle including standard or lightly modified roadsters.

⫸ RECORD BREAKING

The fastest motorcycles of all are the record-breakers: long, low and highly specialized machines built purely to reach phenomenal top speeds in wide open spaces. Aerodynamics are as vital as horsepower at very high speed, and the fastest machines run at places such as the Bonneville salt flats in Utah are streamliners, cigar-shaped projectiles in which the rider reclines with feet forward.

Bikes were much more simple when William Cook took his Peugeot-engined NLG to a recorded 75.9mph (122.14kph) at Brooklands in 1909, setting what is generally accepted as the first speed record. Indian's Jake de Rosier raised the figure to 88.9mph (143.06kph) at the same track two years later, only to be beaten by Matchless founder Charles Collier, who was recorded at 91.3mph (146.92kph) shortly afterwards. In 1920 Indian regained the

crown when Ernie Walker was timed at 104mph (167.36kph) at Daytona Beach. This is regarded as the first official world record, as by now contestants had to make two-way runs within a set time limit.

The 1930s were a great time for record-breaking in Europe, where Germany's Ernst Henne set several new marks on BMWs,

■ OPPOSITE *Bob Leppan at the 1966 London Motorcycle Show in Gyronaut X-1, the twin 650cc engined Triumph on which he set a record of 245.6mph (395.2kph).*

■ LEFT *Don Vesco poses on the Bonneville salt with Lightning Bolt, the twin-engined Kawasaki on which he set a record speed of 318.5mph (512.5kph) in 1978.*

culminating in 173.5mph (279.21kph) in 1937. Henne's great rival was Britain's Eric Fernihough, who earlier the same year had set a 169.7mph (273.09kph) record on his supercharged, JAP-engined Brough Superior. A year later Fernihough was killed when his bike got into a wobble at 180mph (290kph).

The 200mph (321kph) barrier was finally breached in 1956, when Wilhelm Herz

■ ABOVE *Bert Munro's streamlined Munro Special, based on a Model 596 Indian Scout built in 1920, set a class record of 183.5mph (295.3kph) at Bonneville in 1967.*

(427.26kph) on a 1480cc Harley. In 1978 Vesco set a record of 318.5mph (512.5kph) on his Lightning Bolt streamliner, powered by two turbocharged, four-cylinder Kawasaki Z1000 engines. Harley reclaimed the record in 1990 when Dave Campos, riding a twin-engined, 2400cc streamliner – sponsored by readers of the American magazine *Easyriders* – raised the record to 322mph (518.19kph).

■ RIGHT *Bert Le Vack on a Brough Superior SS100 Pendine V-twin, on which he set several speed records in the early 1930s.*

■ BELOW *NSU's 1956 Delphin III's size is emphasized in an aerial shot of the streamliner alongside a conventional racing machine.*

recorded 211.4mph (340.2kph) on a supercharged 500cc NSU. A year earlier Johnny Allen had taken a 650cc Triumph twin to 193.3mph (311kph) at Bonneville. The run was not recognized by the FIM, because no official observers were present, but Allen's exploits led to Triumph's most famous roadster being named the Bonneville.

In recent years the fight on the salt has been between Japan and Harley. American Don Vesco recorded 251.6mph (404.8kph) on a twin-engined, 700cc Yamaha two-stroke streamliner in 1970; a month later fellow road racer Cal Rayborn was timed at 265.5mph

☙ INDEX

Indian ceased production of its Chief V-twin in 1953, but the firm's subsequent attempt to produce British-style parallel twins was unsuccessful.

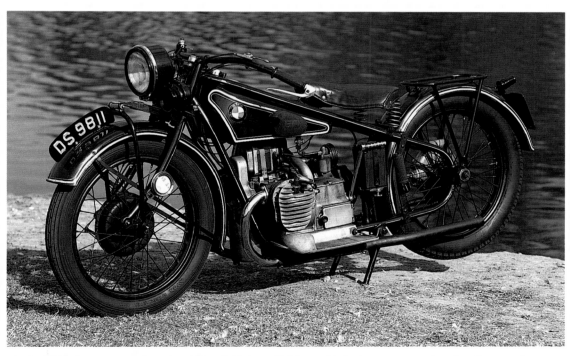

*Early BMW flat-twins, such as this 482cc R52 from 1928, established a reputation for cleanliness and
reliability that the firm would benefit from for many years.*

ACKNOWLEDGEMENTS

The publishers would like to thank the following for their kind permission to reproduce their photographs:

Martyn Barnwell/EMAP and EMAP Archives 10 (all), 11tr, 12tr, 15bl/br, 18b, 19tl, 28b, 37tl/m, 44 (all), 67tl/tr, 68t, 88t, 92t, 93ml. **British Film Institute** 29b, 30 (all), 31t/b. **Roland Brown** Front jacket top middle, 19tr/bl, 21, 22b, 23m, 27b, 33tr, 46b, 53tl/b, 56tr, 57t, 63tmr/tr/b, 78t, 89br, 93mr. **Roland Brown/Gold & Goose** 63tl. **Roland Brown/Phil Masters** 46t, 71tr. **Roland Brown/Mac McDiarmid** 22m, 45b. **Roland Brown/Oli Tennent** Front jacket middle, back jacket flap top, 8, 15t, 19br, 24-5, 27tl, 33b, 59tl, 60b, 61t, 63tl/tml/tmr, 94. **Jack Burnicle** Back jacket bottom right, 82 (all), 83 (all), 84b, 85t. **Kel Edge** 6, 23b, 42-3, 61m, 62, 63m, 77ml, 78b, 81 (all). **John Freeman/(c) Anness Publishing** Back jacket flap top, 36m/tr/b, 37tr. **Gold & Goose** Front jacket top left, back jacket bottom left, 18t, 20t/b, 21t, 48b, 49tr, 52b, 53tl/m, 64-5, 67ml, 72t, 73b, 74-5b, 79t. **Hulton Deutsch Collection** 12tl/b, 16t, 29tl/tr, 45tr, 66 (all), 67b. **Imperial War Museum** 50 (all), 51tl/tr/b. **Phil Masters** Front jacket bottom, jacket front flap, 20m, 21m, 34b, 35t/b, 47tr, 54-5, 60t, 61b. **Mac McDiarmid** 1, 2, 5, 17t/m, 22t, 32b, 37br, 38 (all), 39 (all), 40, 41t/b, 45tl, 48m, 57b, 59tr, 60m, 70b, 71tm, 87t/m, 88b, 89tl/tr/bl, 90t, 96. **Don Morley** Front jacket top right, back jacket top, 4, 3, 8-9, 11tl/m/b, 12m, 13t/b, 14, 16b, 26t, 27tr, 31tl, 32t, 33tl, 34t, 48t, 49tl/b, 51bl, 52t, 53tr, 58tl/tr, 59b, 67mr, 68b, 69tl/tr, 70t, 71tl, 72b, 73tl/tr/m, 75tr, 76t/b, 77tl, 79m/b, 84t, 85b, 86b, 87b, 90b, 91tr, 92b, 93t/b, 95. **Nick Nicholls** 71b, 74t, 75tl, 76m, 77tr/b. **Dick Parnham** 91tl/b. **Garry Stuart** 26b, 28t/m, 46m, 47tl/mr/b. **Oli Tennent** 80. Thanks also to the PR departments of BMW, Ducati, Honda, Moto Guzzi, Kawasaki, Suzuki and Yamaha for their help in supplying photographs, and to Frontiers Motorcycles for the loan of clothing on p36.

t=top, b=bottom, m=middle, l=left, r=right.

Triumph's 650cc Bonneville was the most famous British twin.

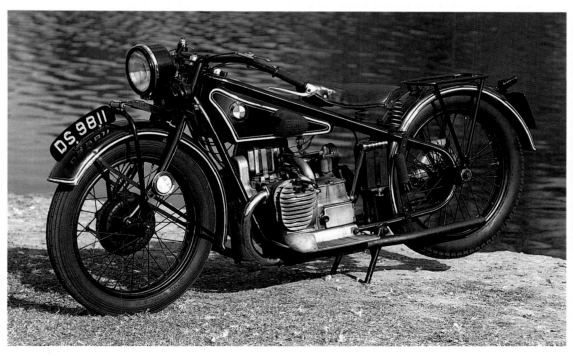

Early BMW flat-twins, such as this 482cc R52 from 1928, established a reputation for cleanliness and reliability that the firm would benefit from for many years.

ACKNOWLEDGEMENTS

The publishers would like to thank the following for their kind permission to reproduce their photographs:

Martyn Barnwell/EMAP and EMAP Archives 10 (all), 11tr, 12tr, 15bl/br, 18b, 19tl, 28b, 37tl/m, 44 (all), 67tl/tr, 68t, 88t, 92t, 93ml. **British Film Institute** 29b, 30 (all), 31t/b. **Roland Brown** Front jacket top middle, 19tr/bl, 21, 22b, 23m, 27b, 33tr, 46b, 53tl/b, 56tr, 57t, 63tmr/tr/b, 78t, 89br, 93mr. **Roland Brown/Gold & Goose** 63tl. **Roland Brown/Phil Masters** 46t, 71tr. **Roland Brown/Mac McDiarmid** 22m, 45b. **Roland Brown/Oli Tennent** Front jacket middle, back jacket flap top, 8, 15t, 19br, 24-5, 27tl, 33b, 59tl, 60b, 61t, 63tl/tml/tmr, 94. **Jack Burnicle** Back

jacket bottom right, 82 (all), 83 (all), 84b, 85t. **Kel Edge** 6, 23b, 42-3, 61m, 62, 63m, 77ml, 78b, 81 (all). **John Freeman/(c) Anness Publishing** Back jacket flap top, 36m/tr/b, 37tr. **Gold & Goose** Front jacket top left, back jacket bottom left, 18t, 20t/b, 21t, 48b, 49tr, 52b, 53tl/m, 64-5, 67ml, 72t, 73b, 74-5b, 79t. **Hulton Deutsch Collection** 12tl/b, 16t, 29tl/tr, 45tr, 66 (all), 67b. **Imperial War Museum** 50 (all), 51tl/tr/b. **Phil Masters** Front jacket bottom, jacket front flap, 20m, 21m, 34b, 35t/b, 47tr, 54-5, 60t, 61b. **Mac McDiarmid** 1, 2, 5, 17t/m, 22t, 32b, 37br, 38 (all), 39 (all), 40, 41t/b, 45tl, 48m, 57b, 59tr, 60m, 70b, 71tm, 87t/m, 88b, 89tl/tr/bl, 90t, 96. **Don Morley** Front jacket top right, back jacket top, 4, 3, 8-9, 11tl/m/b, 12m, 13t/b, 14,

16b, 26t, 27tr, 31tl, 32t, 33tl, 34t, 48t, 49tl/b, 51bl, 52t, 53tr, 58tl/tr, 59b, 67mr, 68b, 69tl/tr, 70t, 71tl, 72b, 73tl/tr/m, 75tr, 76t/b, 77tl, 79m/b, 84t, 85b, 86b, 87b, 90b, 91tr, 92b, 93t/b, 95. **Nick Nicholls** 71b, 74t, 75tl, 76m, 77tr/b. **Dick Parnham** 91tl/b. **Garry Stuart** 26b, 28t/m, 46m, 47tl/mr/b. **Oli Tennent** 80. Thanks also to the PR departments of BMW, Ducati, Honda, Moto Guzzi, Kawasaki, Suzuki and Yamaha for their help in supplying photographs, and to Frontiers Motorcycles for the loan of clothing on p36.

t=top, b=bottom, m=middle, l=left, r=right.

Triumph's 650cc Bonneville was the most famous British twin.